Gemelli

Mostaccioli

Anelli

Rigatoni

Manicotti

Ruote

Conchiglioni

Lasagna
Noodles

Cavatelli

Vermicelli

Better Homes and Gardens®

Low-Fat&Luscious ITALIAN

Better Homes and Gardens® Books
Des Moines, Iowa

Better Homes and Gardens® Books
An imprint of Meredith® Books

Low-Fat & Luscious Italian
Editor: Kristi M. Fuller, R.D.
Contributing Writer: Diane Quagliani, M.B.A., R.D.
Associate Art Director: Lynda Haupert
Contributing Designer: Angie Hoogensen
Copy Chief: Angela K. Renkoski
Editorial and Design Assistants: Judy Bailey,
   Jennifer Norris, Karen Schirm
Test Kitchen Director: Sharon Stilwell
Test Kitchen Product Supervisor: Marilyn Cornelius
Photographers: Mike Dieter, Scott Little
Food Stylists: Lynn Blanchard, Dianna Nolin, Janet Pittman
Electronic Production Coordinator: Paula Forest
Production Manager: Douglas Johnston
Prepress Coordinator: Margie J. Schenkelberg

Director, New Product Development: Ray Wolf
Managing Editor: Christopher Cavanaugh

Meredith® Books
Editor in Chief: Jim Blume
Managing Editor: Christopher Cavanaugh
Director, New Product Development: Ray Wolf

Vice President, General Manager: Jamie L. Martin

Better Homes and Gardens® Magazine
Editor in Chief: Jean LemMon
Executive Food Editor: Nancy Byal
Senior Editor: Joy Taylor
Senior Associate Editors: Jeanne Ambrose, David Feder, R.D.

Meredith® Publishing Group
President, Publishing Group: Christopher Little
Vice President and Publishing Director: John P. Loughlin

Meredith® Corporation
Chairman of the Board and Chief Executive Officer: Jack D. Rehm
President and Chief Operating Officer: William T. Kerr

Chairman of the Executive Committee: E. T. Meredith III

All of us at Better Homes and Gardens® Books are dedicated to providing you with the information and ideas you need to create delicious foods. We welcome your comments and suggestions. Write to us at: Better Homes and Gardens® Books, Cookbook Editorial Department, RW-240, 1716 Locust St., Des Moines, IA 50309-3023.

If you would like to order additional copies of any of our books, check with your local bookstore.

Our seal assures you that every recipe in *Low-Fat & Luscious Italian* has been tested in the Better Homes and Gardens® Test Kitchen. This means that each recipe is practical and reliable, and meets our high standards of taste appeal. We guarantee your satisfaction with this book for as long as you own it.

On the front cover: Vegetable Lasagna with Red Pepper Sauce (see recipe, page 122)
Photo on page 3: Spaghetti and Italian Meatballs (see recipe, page 89)

Low-Fat & Luscious Italian

Italian fare has become so familiar on American tables that it almost *seems* American. But do you often shy away from cooking it for your family because you think it's too high in fat and calories? You don't have to. Authentic Italian dishes aren't necessarily bad for you. Really.

You see, somewhere between sunny Italy and our shores, the healthful essence of traditional Italian cooking was lost. There, heavy cream sauces and large amounts of cheese do not take center stage, and in the old country, meat is reserved for celebrations. Years ago when immigrants came to America, they were encouraged to eat more meat by well-meaning social workers. They were told that their vegetable-rich diet was not good for the digestive system. Many Italians dutifully adopted our more traditional high-meat diet.

Soon, spaghetti was being served with meatballs atop for the first time in its culinary history. Today, as we now know, traditional Italians had the right idea.

True Italian Cuisine

Each of Italy's 20 regions treasures its own distinctive foods and style of cooking. Northern Italy is known for delicate sauces and creamy risottos. Southern Italians covet more highly seasoned dishes and prefer eggless pastas, such as spaghetti. Olive oil, anchovies, and garlic are used more readily to flavor foods in the south than in the north. All Italians enjoy pastas, crusty breads, and fresh produce. Smaller amounts of cheese, meat, poultry, fish and shellfish, and high-flavor accents such as olives, pine nuts, and olive oil round out the menu. Regardless of regional differences, Italians follow one culinary rule: Cook with only fresh, high-quality ingredients. Their adherence to this rule makes their cuisine one of the most healthful in the world.

Now you can savor the flavorful foods of Italy as originally intended. *Low-Fat and Luscious Italian* offers the dishes you love, lightened to reflect the authentic, healthful cooking of Italy. We've reduced the fat, saturated fat, and cholesterol—and kept the flavor—in recipes that are sure to please the health-minded and the discriminating lovers of Italian food.

So, to enjoy the best of health and taste, eat as the Italians do—*buon appetito!*

Contents

Enjoy antipasto—which means "before the meal"—as the Italians do. From caponata to bruschetta, all of the first-course recipes you need to begin a great Italian meal are here.

Italians have a fondness for delicious soups. Here you'll find many to choose from, including a roasted garlic soup, fresh tomato soup, and classic minestrone.

We couldn't forget Italian bread, but you'll also find many other breads, calzones, and all types of pizza.

74 Main Dishes

Familiar classics, such as lasagna, carbonara, and manicotti, can all fit into a nutritious menu. In addition to these, you won't want to miss many of the other favorite Italian entrées.

130 Side Dishes

Don't forget the side dishes. Choose polenta, stuffed artichokes, or eggplant to complement your next Italian meal.

142 Desserts

We've taken sumptuous Italian desserts and pared them down. Serve classic (yet lighter) tiramisu, cheesecake, or zabaglione with no regrets.

Eating Italian Style— To Your Health!

Americans are in love with Italian food. From trendy trattorias to neighborhood spots featuring Mamma's cooking, the number of Italian restaurants is exploding. And whether a restaurant is Italian or not, odds are you'll find at least one Italian-inspired appetizer or entrée on any menu. Hungry seekers of Italian restaurant fare also have increased, doubling in the last five years with no sign of slowing down.

Home cooks are getting into the act, too. Not long ago, their search for Italian ingredients such as balsamic vinegar, arborio rice, and porcini mushrooms meant waiting for mail order or making a trip to a specialty market. Now, thanks to the booming customer demand, a multitude of Italian foods are as close as the corner supermarket. And once-foreign words such as *focaccia, pesto,* and *risotto* are now part of our culinary vocabulary.

Yes, we love the flavors of Italy and want to re-create them in our own kitchens. But in these health-conscious times, we don't want the high-fat price tag that often accompanies the American misinterpretations of Italian cuisine.

If you've given up Italian food or feel guilty about indulging, take heart and enjoy classic Italian dishes—as well as new ones—without consuming too much fat. Authentic Italian fare prepared with fresh, high-quality ingredients is both low-fat and luscious.

Is an Italian diet truly a healthful way of eating for Americans? Yes, because for good health, the U.S. Department of Agriculture's Food Guide Pyramid recommends a diet high in complex carbohydrates and low in fat—a perfect match for Italian-style eating. The examples below show how typical Italian foods fit perfectly into the pyramid. Turn to Favorite Italian Ingredients on page 10 for descriptions and tips on buying and using the freshest ingredients.

Eating Italian—Pyramid Style

Grains: Focaccia, pizza crust, polenta, bread sticks, risotto, gnocchi, Italian bread, pasta

Vegetables: Tomatoes, asparagus, spinach, squash, zucchini, broccoli, mixed greens, artichokes, onions, eggplant, squash, mushrooms, marinara or spaghetti sauce, sweet peppers

Fruits: Raisins, dried fruits, melons, raspberries, blueberries, strawberries, pomegranates

Meat (choose lean meat): Chicken, pork, sausage, veal, beef, fish, seafood; cooked garbanzo and cannellini beans; lentils

Dairy products (choose reduced-fat products): Gelato, yogurt, milk, cheeses (such as Parmesan, ricotta, mozzarella, Asiago)

Fats, oils, and sweets (eat in moderation): Olives, butter, margarine, oils (such as olive oil), chocolate, pine nuts, Italian ice, whipped cream

What You'll Find in This Book

Thanks to the nutrition analyses provided in this book, it's easy to see the amount of fat (in grams) and the Percent Daily Value Fat in each recipe. Here are the Nutrition Facts listed with every recipe:

TOTAL FAT: 11 g
DAILY VALUE FAT: 17%
SATURATED FAT: 2
DAILY VALUE SATURATED FAT: 10%

NUTRITION FACTS PER SERVING:

Calories	370
Total Fat	11 g
Saturated Fat	2 g
Cholesterol	45 mg
Sodium	563 mg
Carbohydrate	48 g
Fiber	2 g
Protein	22 g

In this book, and on today's food labels, the Percent Daily Value Fat is based on a daily intake of 2,000 calories and 65 grams fat (including 20 grams saturated fat). In the above example, you can see that this recipe includes 11 grams of fat (17% of the 65 fat grams for the day) and 2 grams saturated fat (10% of the 20 grams saturated fat for the day).

Determining Your Fat Budget

To translate 30 percent calories from fat to fat grams, take the number of calories you need in a day, multiply by 30 percent (or 0.3), and divide by 9 (the number of calories in 1 gram of fat):

Daily calories	Your Daily Fat Budget
1,200	40 grams
1,600	53 grams
1,800	60 grams
2,000	67 grams*

*Note: *Guidelines on food labels are based on 2,000 calories a day. The fat grams, based on the recommendation of no more than 30% of calories from fat, are rounded off to 65 on all food labels.*

Making Flavorful and Healthful
Italian Meals

To create the flavors of Italy in your own kitchen, select the freshest ingredients you can afford. Buy fruits and vegetables in season, check to make sure meats and fish are fresh with no signs of spoilage, and look for natural cheeses that are free from molds. Then follow these tips for high-flavor, low-fat cooking:

● Select strong-flavored hard cheeses such as Parmesan and Romano. Grate them extra fine to make a small amount go further.
● Substitute reduced-fat or fat-free cheeses, such as mozzarella and ricotta, for regular types in your favorite lasagna recipe.
● Use extra-virgin olive oil to complement the flavor of raw or finished dishes such as salads, soups, and focaccias. Because of its fruity flavor, a drizzle is all you need.
● Roast vegetables tossed in a small amount of olive oil to intensify their flavor.

● Use sun-dried tomatoes and dried porcini mushrooms to add intense flavor to dishes without adding fat.
● Top pizza, focaccia, and sandwiches with roasted red, green, and yellow peppers for high-impact color and flavor.
● Use fresh and dried spices and herbs to add flavor without fat or salt.
● Toast pine nuts and other nuts before adding them to the recipe. Toasting brings out their rich flavor so you can use fewer of them.

Health Myths and Facts About Italian Food

Myth: *Pasta is fattening.*

Fact: Pasta, a mainstay in the Italian diet, is not fattening. A 2-ounce serving (1 cup cooked) of dry pasta, such as spaghetti, contains just under 200 calories and less than 1 gram of fat. When it comes to calories and fat, it's what's on top that counts. Rich, creamy sauces or sauces full of fatty ingredients such as sausage or cheese can send the calorie and fat total in your pasta dish sky-high. Choose vegetable-based sauces (such as Tomato-Sauced Penne with Meatballs, page 88, or Fish Fillets with Red Pepper Sauce, page 106) to keep calories and fat low.

Myth: *Eating plenty of olive oil will protect me from heart disease.*

Fact: Olive oil is a monounsaturated fat that can help lower blood cholesterol if it is *substituted* for saturated fats, which are plentiful in fatty meats, whole milk products, and coconut, palm, and palm kernel oils. But to reduce blood cholesterol and risk of heart disease, the American Heart Association recommends keeping the total amount of fat you eat within bounds. All types of fat, including olive oil, should make up no more than 30 percent of the calories you eat in a day.

If you're watching the scale, keep in mind that all oils, including olive oil, contain about 120 calories per tablespoon. Eating large amounts of calorie-rich olive oil can result in weight gain, and being overweight puts you at risk for heart disease.

Small amounts of olive oil are used in some recipes in this book to enhance the authentic Italian flavor of these dishes. See the Glossary (page 10) to learn about the different types of olive oils.

Myth: *If I drink wine every day as the Italians do, I can eat whatever I want and stay healthy.*

Fact: Drinking wine is not a cure-all for bad eating habits. However, current research suggests that drinking a moderate amount of red wine each day while following a low-fat, high-fiber eating plan may reduce risk of heart disease. (A moderate amount of wine is no more than one 5-ounce glass for women and two 5-ounce glasses for men.) If you are a healthy, nonpregnant adult and your waistline can afford the extra 100 calories per glass, do as the Italians do and enjoy a glass of vino with your meals.

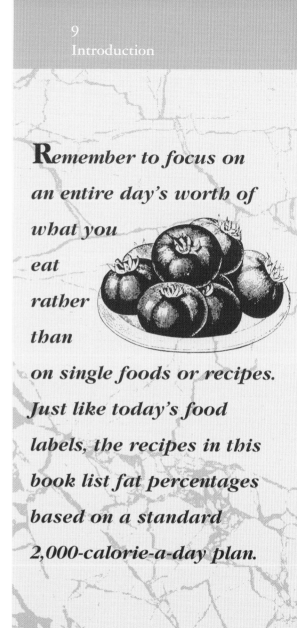

Remember to focus on an entire day's worth of what you eat rather than on single foods or recipes. Just like today's food labels, the recipes in this book list fat percentages based on a standard 2,000-calorie-a-day plan.

Pasta Pluses

Pasta isn't fattening.

It's the toppers that can add

lots of calories and fat, so choose

sauces that aren't heavy in oils,

cream, or cheeses. Try lighter

sauces, such as the tomato-based

types found on pages 88 and 89.

Favorite Italian Ingredients

Arborio rice. Risotto is traditionally made with this Italian rice, although other rices can be used. Risotto is Arborio rice that is browned first in margarine, butter, or oil, then cooked in broth. The finished rice has a creamy consistency and a tender, but slightly firm, texture.

Artichokes. Look for firm, compact globes that are heavy for their size. They should yield slightly to pressure and have large, tightly closed leaves. (Sometimes leaf edges darken because the plant got too cold. This darkening, called "winter kiss," does not affect the quality.) To store, place fresh artichokes in a plastic bag and refrigerate for up to a week.

To prepare an artichoke, cut off the bottom stem so it sits flat. Cut off about 1 inch from the top. Remove loose outer leaves. With kitchen shears, snip ½ inch from tips of leaves. Brush cut surfaces with lemon juice to prevent browning. You can remove the fuzzy choke with a grapefruit knife or spoon.

Balsamic vinegar. This sweet, dark brown vinegar is made from the boiled-down juice of a white grape. According to Italian law, balsamic vinegars labeled as *aceto balsaminco tradizionale* cannot contain any wine vinegar and must be aged at least 12 years. These vinegars can sell for $40 to $350 for 4 ounces. Less expensive balsamics blend wine vinegar with the grape juice.

Basil. The aroma and flavor of this herb range from peppery and robust to sweet and spicy. Its leaves can be various shades of green or purple. Use the leaves of this herb in dried or fresh form.

Cheeses

Cooking cheeses

Ricotta: Ricotta is generally made from cow's milk, although it can be made with sheep's milk, which has more flavor. It's not readily available in the United States. Ricotta is characteristically a bit grainy in texture with a mildly sweet flavor. It can be found in lower-fat versions at the supermarket. Depending on whether the milk used in making the ricotta was whole or skim, the fat content of ½ cup (4 ounces) ranges from 0 to 15 grams.

Mozzarella: Best known as a pizza topper, mozzarella is made either from cow's milk or, in Italy, from water buffalo's milk. It is mild in flavor and can be found in lower-fat varieties. Fresh mozzarella, a real treat, is made from whole milk and has a softer texture and sweeter, more delicate flavor than regular, factory-made mozzarella. It contains from 4 to 7 grams of fat per ounce, depending on the fat content of the milk used to make it.

Grating cheeses

Pecorino: Made from sheep's milk, the flavor of pecorino will depend on the area where it is made in Italy. It ranges from a firm, sharp, salty cheese to a milder, semifirm variety. It has 8 grams of fat per ounce.

Parmesan cheese: Parmigiano-Reggiano cheese, an aged hard cheese made from cow's milk, is strictly regulated in Italy to control its quality. In the United States, this cheese often is imitated, but the results are different from the Italian cheese. Older, aged varieties of Italy have a stronger flavor and are drier. Stick to freshly grated aged varieties for the most flavor. You'll be able to use less due to its more intense flavor. It contains 7 grams fat per ounce.

Table cheeses

Asiago cheese: Made from cow's milk, Asiago is a semihard to hard cheese. Full of many tiny holes, the cheese has a rich flavor and creamy texture when it hasn't been aged for very long. As it ages, the cheese becomes firmer and can be grated easily. It is similar in fat content to Parmesan cheese.

Fontina: This delicate, sweet, semisoft cheese has a nutty flavor. Made from cow's milk, fontina melts easily and smoothly. The more aged the cheese, the richer the flavor. One ounce has about 9 grams fat.

Gorgonzola: This blue-veined cheese is named for a town near Milan where the cheese originated. It is made from cow's milk and possesses a creamy texture with a slightly pungent, rich flavor. When aged for more than 6 months, the flavor can become very strong. It's a great accompaniment to fruit, such as apples or pears. It also can be melted into sauces or crumbled over salads. For a milder variety, look for *torta di Gorgonzola,* which layers Gorgonzola with sweet mascarpone. Gorgonzola cheese has 8 grams of fat per ounce.

Mascarpone: Super-rich mascarpone tastes like a cross between whipped butter and cream cheese. It is often used in desserts, but it's also great as a spread for fresh fruit, such as strawberries or pear slices, or delicate crackers. It is a soft cheese made from cow's milk and has about 13 grams fat per ounce—use sparingly.

Provolone: Made from cow's milk, this cheese is delicate and creamy when aged for up to two months. When aged longer, it begins to take on a spicy, sharp flavor. Although it's great as a table cheese, provolone is also an excellent cooking cheese. Aged provolone can be used for grating. One ounce has about 8 grams fat.

Cheeses of Italy

Compare cheeses (per 1-ounce serving) for the best fat and calorie bargains.

	Calories	Fat (grams)
Asiago	110	7
Goat cheese	76	6
Fontina	110	9
Gorgonzola	100	8
Mascarpone	124	13
Mozzarella		
skim milk	72	5
whole milk	80	6
Parmesan	110	7
Pecorino	110	7
Provolone	100	8
Ricotta		
whole milk	50	4
part-skim milk	40	2
no-fat milk	20	0
Romano	110	8

For Good Measure

When you make pasta, do you ever end up with too much or too little for the number of people you're serving? Follow these guidelines to end up with just the right amount.

- **8 ounces uncooked small to medium dried pasta shapes (such as farfalle or bow ties, elbow macaroni, or penne) = 4 cups cooked (4 servings)**

- **8 ounces uncooked dried long pasta shapes (such as linguine, fettuccine, or spaghetti) = a 1½-inch-diameter bunch = 4 cups cooked (4 servings)**

- **8 ounces uncooked dried egg noodles = 2½ cups cooked (2 to 3 servings)**

Garlic. The plant of this strong-scented, pungent bulb is related to the onion. Besides fresh garlic bulbs, you also can find dried and bottled minced garlic, garlic juice, garlic powder, garlic salt, and garlic paste. *Test Kitchen Tip:* Store garlic heads in a cool, dry, dark place. Leave bulbs whole, as individual cloves dry out quickly. Keep any dried garlic products in a cool, dry, dark place and use within 6 months. Store the bottled minced garlic in the refrigerator for up to 6 months.

Italian parsley. Italian parsley has flat, dark leaves and a milder flavor than the more familiar curly-leaf parsley.

Mushrooms. Porcini, the most prized wild mushrooms in Italy, have large, meaty, slightly rounded caps that may be white to reddish brown. The stems are fleshy and wider at the bottom. Another mushroom in Italy is the crimini (Italian brown or Roman), which has the same shape as a regular button mushroom but is light tan to dark brown with a deeper, earthier flavor.

To clean, brush mushrooms with a soft brush or damp paper towel. Store them in a paper bag until ready to use. Serve them within a couple of days. If you have trouble finding a specific kind, look for the dried form. Add fresh or rehydrated mushrooms to soups, sauces, salads, appetizers, pasta dishes, and entrées.

Olive oil. The quality of olive oil is classified by the level of acidity, taste, and aroma. Olive oils higher in acidity can be rectified, or treated with chemicals to lower the acidity, but are called refined, not virgin.

Olive oil has the same amount of calories that other oils contain—120 calories per tablespoon. But olive oil is highly unsaturated and has been suggested as a healthier alternative to more saturated fat or oils. Additionally, olive oil is a highly flavored oil, so you can use much less than oils with lighter flavors.

Extra-virgin olive oil is the best grade of olive oil; it meets Italy's highest standards for rich and fruity olive taste with very low acidity (less than 1 percent).

Virgin olive oil has an acidity between 1 and 3 percent and a ligher taste and aroma. It is considered to be slightly inferior in quality to extra-virgin olive oil.

Pure olive oil is filtered twice after a single cold-pressing to lighten the oil's color and aroma and lessen the acidity. It has a delicate flavor and a low acidity.

Cold-pressed olive oil is obtained by pressing the fruit. No heat or solvents are used, therefore it is called "cold-pressed."

Extra-light olive oil refers only to the oil's flavor, not to the calories it contains compared to the other olive oils.

continued

Test Kitchen Tip: Store olive oil in a tightly capped container in a cool, dark place. It does not need to be refrigerated, but it may be stored in the refrigerator during hot, humid weather. Tightly capped olive oil will keep for several years.

Olives. Italians prefer to use ripe olives rather than the unripe green variety. Although ripe olives in America are usually black, the color of Italian ripe olives can vary from purplish red and brown to jet-black. They are packed in oil or brine, which may be flavored with herbs or citrus peel. Taste olives before serving. If they're too salty, rinse them under cold running water. They can become bitter if overcooked, so allow them just enough time to heat through when adding to a cooked dish.

Pancetta (pan-CHEH-tuh). Think of pancetta as the Italian version of bacon. Made from the belly or *pancia* of a hog, pancetta has deep pink stripes of flesh similar to bacon. Pancetta is seasoned with pepper and other spices, is cured with salt, but is not smoked. It comes in a sausagelike roll or flat and is used to flavor sauces, vegetables, or meats.

Pesto (PES-toh). A pasty sauce of olive oil, garlic, fresh basil, and Parmesan cheese. It usually is served with pasta.

Pine nuts or pignoli. This small seed is from one of the several pine tree varieties. The pine nut, which has a sweet, faint pine flavor, also is known as pignoli and piñon. The small, creamy white nut can be slender and pellet-shaped or more triangular. Pine nuts turn rancid quickly, so refrigerate them in an airtight container for up to 2 months or freeze them for up to 6 months.

Polenta (poh-LEN-tuh). This Italian-style mush is made by boiling a mixture of cornmeal or farina and water. Polenta usually is served with tomato sauce as a side dish, or it may be served without sauce as a bread substitute. It is eaten as a thick porridge or can be molded, sliced, fried, or broiled.

Prosciutto (proh-SHOO-toh). Like ham, prosciutto is from the hog's leg. Salt-curing draws out the moisture, a process called *prosciugare* in Italian. Unlike ham, the cured pork is air-dried not smoked. The result is a somewhat sweetly spiced, rose-colored meat that has a slight sheen.

Parma ham is the authentic proscuitto of Italy. They are designated as prosciutto cotto (cooked) or prosciutto crudo (raw). The raw is cured, however, so it is ready to eat. Use small amounts in pasta, sauces, and meat dishes. Add it to cooked dishes at the last minute so it doesn't toughen.

How Much to Make?

● **When cooking homemade or refrigerated pasta, plan on 4 ounces for each main-dish serving and 2 ounces for each side-dish serving.**

● **When cooking packaged dried pasta, use 2 ounces for each main-dish serving and 1 ounce for each side-dish serving.**

The Perfect Match—
Pairing Your Pasta and Sauce

Certain pasta shapes work best with certain sauces. Follow these suggestions:

● When you're serving a smooth sauce such as a velvety tomato or a creamy Alfredo, choose flat pastas such as linguini or fettuccine that the sauce will cling to and coat.

● Match light, delicate sauces such as fresh tomato basil with delicate pastas such as angel hair or thin spaghetti.

● If your sauce is chunky with bits of vegetables, meat, poultry, or seafood, capture every chunk by choosing a shaped pasta such as farfalle (bow ties) or shells, or a tube-shaped pasta such as penne or ziti.

Risotto (ree-ZOHT-toh). This rice dish consists of broth-cooked rice, butter, cheese, and other bits of meat and/or vegetables that are available. *Risotto Milanese* (from Milan) is always additionally flavored with a little saffron.

Tomatoes. Italian cooks mainly use two kinds of tomatoes. They like elongated plum or Roma tomatoes for cooking, because they have fewer seeds, firmer flesh, and thicker juice. The round eating tomatoes are prized in salads, appetizers, or anywhere fresh tomatoes are needed.

To ripen, store firm tomatoes at room temperature in a brown paper bag. When ripe, they will yield to gentle pressure.

Perfect Pasta Every Time

Italians describe perfectly cooked pasta as *al dente,* which means "to the tooth." Pasta cooked al dente is tender but still slightly firm when bitten. For al dente pasta every time, follow these tips:

To cook 8 ounces of dried pasta, bring 2 to 4 quarts of water to a rolling boil in a large saucepan or kettle. (You can divide this recipe according to the amount of pasta you are cooking.) If desired, add a little salt and olive oil or cooking oil to help keep the pasta separated.

Add the pasta a little at a time so the water does not stop boiling. Hold long pasta, such as spaghetti, at one end and dip the other end into the water. As the pasta softens, gently curl it around the pan and down into the water.

Stir the pasta when you first add it to the water and occasionally during cooking.

Reduce the heat slightly and boil the pasta, uncovered, for the time specified on the package, or until the pasta is al dente. Use a long-handled fork or spoon to test the pasta often for doneness near the end of the specified cooking time.

Drain pasta in a colander. Serve immediately with sauce.

The Italian Menu

Plan an Italian meal as the Italians would. Set the theme for your meal with a familiar Italian dish or an interesting new entrée, then build the meal around it. Select foods that complement each other—one food shouldn't overwhelm the rest. Whenever you're planning meals (not just Italian), consider the compatibility of textures, colors, and flavors. For example, serve a crisp-textured side dish with a soft-textured main dish, contrast a mild first course with a zesty second course, balance a hot food with a cold accompaniment, and serve a less colorful food with a bright partner. Plan a lighter dessert to finish a heartier meal.

Even the simplest Italian meal is composed of at least two courses. The first course, usually pasta, risotto, or soup, is followed by a second course of meat, poultry, fish, or seafood. Follow the sequence of courses outlined below to round out a meal in the Italian style.

Pasta is a popular choice for the first course (*primo piatto*). Pasta is versatile—it can be tossed, baked, or stuffed with a variety of fresh ingredients or topped with many different sauces.

The second course (*secondo piatto*) of meat, poultry, fish, or seafood is presented with at least one and sometimes two vegetable side dishes. A crisp garden salad may take the place of a vegetable dish, although Italians sometimes serve salad after the second course. Breadsticks or crusty Italian bread and a glass of wine may complete the second course. Popular red wines include Chianti, Lambrusco, Bardolino, valpolicella, barbaresco, and Barolo. Popular white wines include frascati and Soave.

Dessert, fruit, and/or cheese courses follow the last or second course. A sweet dessert wine, such as port, Tokay, cream sherry, or Marsala, may be served. Italians usually conclude the meal with a tiny cup of full-bodied espresso coffee.

Meals for special occasions are more elaborate and often begin with an antipasto course. Antipasto means "before the meal." The course consists of a blend of meat, fish, seafood, vegetable, and/or fruit appetizers. The antipasto often is accompanied by a light wine.
(For Italian menu suggestions, see pages 154 and 155.)

Storing and Freezing Pasta

● Store dried, uncooked pasta unopened in its original package or in a sealed storage bag in a cool, dry place. It will last almost indefinitely.

● Store fresh or refrigerated pasta in an airtight container in the refrigerator for up to 5 days or in the freezer for up to 8 months.

● Keep frozen pasta in the freezer for up to 8 months.

● Refrigerate leftover pasta in an airtight container for up to 5 days. Pasta will continue to absorb flavors and oils from sauces, so store cooked pasta and sauce separately.

Marinated Vegetables Salad, recipe on page 19

Spinach-Cheese Tart,
recipe on page 22

Appetizers

You won't be without low-fat appetizers when you plan your Italian menu because we've included all your favorites, such as Caponata (page 30) and Bruschetta with Goat Cheese (page 24). Or, try Panzanella (page 18), a delicious bread salad, or Polenta with Tomato-Mushroom Sauce (page 29) just before your meal. Whatever you choose, you'll know that it's good for you *and* tastes great.

Panzanella

Use a hearty, dark bread, such as Country Whole Wheat Bread (see recipe, page 58), that is a few days old. Using bread that is too fresh will cause your salad to be soggy.

3 cups torn bite-size pieces (or 1-inch cubes) day-old Italian or wheat bread

1 pound tomatoes, seeded and coarsely chopped

½ of a medium red onion, cut into thin wedges and separated

½ of a small cucumber, peeled and cut into chunks

¼ cup snipped fresh basil

2 tablespoons snipped parsley

2 cloves garlic, minced

2 tablespoons red or white wine vinegar

2 tablespoons olive oil

¼ teaspoon salt

⅛ teaspoon pepper

Torn mixed greens (about 4 cups)

● In a large mixing bowl combine the bread pieces, tomatoes, onion, cucumber, basil, parsley, and minced garlic.

● For dressing, in a small bowl stir together the vinegar, oil, salt, and pepper. Spoon the dressing over the bread mixture, tossing gently to coat. Let stand about 15 minutes to allow flavors to blend. Serve dressing over torn mixed greens. Makes 4 servings.

Marinated Vegetables Salad

Balsamic vinegar, made from white Trebbiano grape juice, adds a sweet flavor to this salad. This type of vinegar is aged in wooden barrels for at least 10 years, making it more expensive than other vinegars. (Pictured on page 16.)

2 medium ripe fresh tomatoes or
  4 Roma tomatoes
1 medium green pepper
1 small zucchini or yellow summer squash,
  thinly sliced (1¼ cups)
¼ cup thinly sliced red onion
2 tablespoons snipped parsley
2 tablespoons olive oil
2 tablespoons balsamic or wine vinegar
2 tablespoons water
1 tablespoon snipped fresh thyme or basil,
  or 1 teaspoon dried thyme or basil,
  crushed
1 clove garlic, minced
1 tablespoon pine nuts, toasted (optional)

● Cut tomatoes into wedges. Cut green pepper into small squares. In a large bowl combine tomatoes, green pepper, zucchini or summer squash, onion, and parsley.

● For dressing, in a screw-top jar combine oil, vinegar, water, thyme or basil, and garlic. Cover and shake well. Pour dressing over vegetable mixture. Toss lightly to coat.

● Let mixture stand at room temperature for 30 to 60 minutes, stirring occasionally. (Or, cover and refrigerate for 4 to 24 hours, stirring once or twice. Allow to stand at room temperature about 30 minutes before serving.) If desired, stir in the pine nuts. Serve with slotted spoon. Makes 6 to 8 servings.

A Toast to Nuts

Although nuts can be high in fat and calories, when used sparingly, they add flavor and crunch to a dish without breaking your fat budget. Toasting makes nuts even more flavorful and helps keep them crisp even in sauces and other moist mixtures. To toast nuts, place them in a shallow baking pan; bake in a 400° oven for 7 to 8 minutes or until they start to brown. Make more than you need and freeze the leftovers in an airtight container for use later.

TOTAL FAT: 2 g
DAILY VALUE FAT: 3%
SATURATED FAT: 0 g
DAILY VALUE SATURATED FAT: 0%

NUTRITION FACTS
PER SERVING:

Calories	41
Total Fat	2 g
Saturated Fat	0 g
Cholesterol	0 mg
Sodium	6 mg
Carbohydrate	5 g
Fiber	1 g
Protein	1 g

EXCHANGES:
1 Vegetable
½ Fat

PREPARATION TIME: 20 minutes
STANDING TIME: 30 minutes

Roasted Sweet Pepper Salad

Use any leftovers of this flavorful salad for an extra-special sandwich topping. It's especially tasty on a grilled chicken sandwich.

6 medium red, yellow, and/or green
    sweet peppers, halved lengthwise,
    stems, seeds, and membranes removed
3 tablespoons balsamic vinegar
2 tablespoons capers, drained
2 tablespoons snipped fresh basil or
    1 teaspoon dried basil, crushed
1 tablespoon olive oil
1 tablespoon snipped fresh oregano or
    1 teaspoon dried oregano, crushed
2 cloves garlic, minced
¼ teaspoon ground black pepper
    Lettuce leaves

● Place sweet pepper halves, cut sides down, on a baking sheet lined with foil. Bake in a 425° oven about 20 minutes or until dark and bubbly. Cover peppers or wrap in foil about 10 minutes. Peel; cut into strips.

● In a medium bowl combine sweet peppers, vinegar, capers, basil, oil, oregano, garlic, and pepper; toss to coat. Serve immediately or cover and chill up to 24 hours. Serve on salad plates lined with lettuce. Makes 6 to 8 servings.

TOTAL FAT: 3 g
DAILY VALUE FAT: 4%
SATURATED FAT: 0 g
DAILY VALUE SATURATED FAT: 0%

NUTRITION FACTS
PER SERVING:

Calories	58
Total Fat	3 g
Saturated Fat	0 g
Cholesterol	0 mg
Sodium	55 mg
Carbohydrate	9 g
Fiber	3 g
Protein	1 g

EXCHANGES:
1½ Vegetable
½ Fat

START TO FINISH: 55 minutes

TOTAL FAT: 7 g
DAILY VALUE FAT: 10%
SATURATED FAT: 3 g
DAILY VALUE SATURATED FAT: 15%

NUTRITION FACTS
PER SERVING:

Calories	142
Total Fat	7 g
Saturated Fat	3 g
Cholesterol	46 mg
Sodium	112 mg
Carbohydrate	12 g
Fiber	1 g
Protein	6 g

EXCHANGES:
½ Starch
1 Vegetable
½ Medium-Fat Meat
1 Fat

PREPARATION TIME: 25 minutes
COOKING TIME: 25 minutes

Spinach-Cheese Tart

Using oil instead of shortening or butter in the pastry dough keeps saturated fat low. Try a fruity olive oil for added flavor. (Pictured on pages 16 and 17.)

1 **Pastry Shell**
2 **eggs**
1 **cup low-fat ricotta cheese**
½ **cup crumbled semisoft goat cheese**
¼ **cup skim milk**
½ **cup chopped fresh spinach**
¼ **cup chopped, well drained, canned roasted red sweet peppers**
2 **teaspoons snipped fresh oregano or ¾ teaspoon dried oregano, crushed**
1 **small red or yellow sweet pepper, cut into strips (optional)**
   Fresh oregano (optional)

● Prepare Pastry Shell. On a lightly floured surface flatten the ball of dough with your hands. Roll out from the center to the edge, forming a 12-inch circle.

● Ease pastry into a 9½- or 10-inch tart pan with a removable bottom, being careful not to stretch the pastry. Trim pastry even with rim of pan. Do not prick. Line pastry with a double thickness of heavy foil. Bake in a 450° oven for 10 to 12 minutes or until edge is golden. Remove from oven. Reduce oven temperature to 325°.

● Meanwhile, in a medium mixing bowl beat eggs slightly with an electric mixer. Add ricotta cheese, goat cheese, and milk. Beat until smooth. Stir in spinach, roasted sweet peppers, and the fresh or dried oregano. Pour egg mixture into pastry. Bake in a 325° oven about 20 minutes or until a knife inserted near the center comes out clean.

● Let stand about 5 minutes. If desired, top with sweet pepper strips and additional fresh oregano. Makes 12 servings.

Pastry Shell: In a medium mixing bowl stir together 1¼ cups *all-purpose flour* and ¼ teaspoon *salt*. In a 1-cup measure combine ¼ cup *skim milk* and 3 tablespoons *cooking oil*. Add oil mixture all at once to flour mixture. Stir with a fork until dough forms a ball.

Eggplant with
Herbed Goat Cheese

Fresh eggplant is available year-round. Select plump, glossy, heavy eggplants without any scarred, bruised, or dull surfaces. Salting them as we do here draws out any bitter flavor.

1 **small eggplant (about 12 ounces)**
1 **5½- or 6-ounce package soft goat cheese (chèvre)**
1 **tablespoon snipped fresh basil**
  or 1 teaspoon dried basil, crushed
1 **teaspoon onion powder**
  Dash ground black pepper
1 **tablespoon milk (optional)**
2 **tablespoons olive oil**
  Lemon-pepper seasoning or ground black pepper
1 **small tomato, seeded and chopped**
  Snipped fresh basil

● Wash eggplant; do not peel. Cut the eggplant crosswise into about sixteen ½-inch slices. Sprinkle each side of the eggplant slices lightly with salt. Place them on paper towels; let stand for 20 minutes. Blot the surfaces of the slices with paper towels.

● In a small bowl combine the cheese, the 1 tablespoon basil, onion powder, and dash pepper. If mixture seems dry, add some of the milk. Cover and chill until needed (can be made ahead and chilled for up to 1 day).

● Brush the eggplant slices with oil. Place the eggplant in a single layer on an unheated rack of a broiler pan. Broil 4 to 5 inches from the heat for 5 minutes. Turn; broil 3 to 4 minutes more or until tender.

● Remove eggplant slices from oven and spread with the cheese mixture. Sprinkle with lemon-pepper seasoning or pepper. Broil for about 1 minute more or until cheese is heated through.

● To serve, top each with chopped tomato and additional snipped basil. Makes 16 servings.

Cheese from a Goat

The distinctive tangy flavor of goat cheese adds kick to appetizers, salads, and meat dishes. Soft goat cheese, or chèvre, can be used in dips and spreads. But be careful not to beat it or it will break down. For recipes that require the goat cheese be sliced, crumbled, cubed, or shaped into rounds, choose a semisoft type.

TOTAL FAT: 5 g
DAILY VALUE FAT: 7%
SATURATED FAT: 2 g
DAILY VALUE SATURATED FAT: 10%

NUTRITION FACTS
PER SERVING:

Calories	58
Total Fat	5 g
Saturated Fat	2 g
Cholesterol	8 mg
Sodium	88 mg
Carbohydrate	2 g
Fiber	1 g
Protein	2 g

EXCHANGES:
½ Vegetable
1 Fat

PREPARATION TIME: 30 minutes
COOKING TIME: 9 minutes

TOTAL FAT: 3 g
DAILY VALUE FAT: 4%
SATURATED FAT: 1 g
DAILY VALUE SATURATED FAT: 5%

NUTRITION FACTS
PER SERVING:

Calories	57
Total Fat	3 g
Saturated Fat	1 g
Cholesterol	5 mg
Sodium	94 mg
Carbohydrate	5 g
Fiber	1 g
Protein	2 g

EXCHANGES:
½ **Starch**
½ **Fat**

START TO FINISH: 30 minutes

Bruschetta with Goat Cheese

Bruschetta (broo-SHEH-tah or broo-SKEH-tah) is toasted bread, traditionally rubbed with garlic and drizzled with olive oil. Our version combines two cheeses, sweet red peppers, and olives. (Pictured at top of photo.)

1 **8-ounce loaf baguette-style French bread**
2 **tablespoons olive oil**
3 **ounces semisoft goat cheese, crumbled**
2 **ounces light cream cheese (Neufchâtel)**
2 **teaspoons lemon juice**
1 **teaspoon snipped fresh sage or oregano**
     or ¼ teaspoon ground sage or oregano
1 **7-ounce jar roasted red sweet peppers,**
     drained
¼ **cup coarsely chopped pitted Italian or**
     ripe olives
½ **teaspoon olive oil**
     Small fresh sage or oregano leaves
     (optional)

● Cut bread into ½-inch-thick slices. Lightly brush both sides of the bread slices with the 2 tablespoons oil. Arrange slices on an ungreased baking sheet.

● Bake in a 425° oven about 10 minutes or until crisp and light brown, turning once. (If desired, transfer the cooled toasts to a storage container. Cover and store at room temperature for up to 24 hours.)

● Meanwhile, in a medium bowl stir together the goat cheese, cream cheese, lemon juice, and snipped sage or oregano. Cut the sweet peppers into strips. Toss olives with the ½ teaspoon oil.

● To assemble, spread toast with cheese mixture. Top with red pepper strips, chopped olives, and, if desired, sage or oregano leaves. Serve warm or at room temperature. To heat, return slices to the ungreased baking sheet. Bake in a 425° oven about 3 minutes or until the toppings are heated through. Makes about 24.

Clockwise from top: Bruschetta with Goat Cheese *(recipe above),* Caponata *(recipe on page 30),* and Lemon-Olive Spread *(recipe on page 31)*

TOTAL FAT: 3 g
DAILY VALUE FAT: 4%
SATURATED FAT: 0 g
DAILY VALUE SATURATED FAT: 0%

NUTRITION FACTS
PER SERVING:

Calories	39
Total Fat	3 g
Saturated Fat	0 g
Cholesterol	0 mg
Sodium	78 mg
Carbohydrate	4 g
Fiber	1 g
Protein	1 g

EXCHANGES:
1 Vegetable
½ Fat

PREPARATION TIME: 10 minutes
COOKING TIME: 8 minutes

Broiled Portobello Mushrooms

Try these meaty mushrooms in a sandwich with ripe tomato slices and chopped fresh basil.

2   **extra-large portobello mushrooms**
2   **cloves garlic, minced**
¼   **to ½ teaspoon crushed red pepper (optional)**
¼   **teaspoon seasoned salt**
2   **teaspoons olive oil**
1   **tablespoon snipped fresh basil**

● Remove the stems from the mushrooms. Wipe mushrooms with a clean, damp cloth or paper towel. Place clean mushrooms, stem side up, in a small shallow baking pan. Set aside.

● In a small bowl combine the garlic, red pepper (if desired), and seasoned salt. Divide the mixture in half; sprinkle each mushroom evenly with half of the mixture. Drizzle 1 teaspoon of the oil over each mushroom.

● Broil mushrooms 3 to 4 inches from the heat for 8 to 10 minutes or until tender. Sprinkle with the fresh basil. Serve immediately. Makes 4 to 6 servings.

Portly Portobellos

Have you wondered about those oversize mushrooms that are appearing on the grocery shelves? Portobello mushrooms are mature brown mushrooms with a hearty beef flavor that intensifies with cooking. As with other mushrooms, the specimens you choose should be firm, with dry gills and no soft spots on the cap. Refrigerate them, unwashed and in paper bags, or with a paper towel in a porous plastic bag. They'll keep this way for several days to a week.

Potato Croquettes
Stuffed with Cheese

Croquettes usually are deep-fried. Our baked version has only 4 grams of fat per serving.

3 medium potatoes, peeled and quartered
1 beaten egg or ¼ cup refrigerated or
   frozen egg product, thawed
2 ounces prosciutto or lean cooked ham,
   diced (about ½ cup)
¼ cup grated Parmesan or Romano cheese
1 tablespoon snipped fresh basil
3 ounces part-skim mozzarella cheese, cut
   into 18 cubes
¾ cup fine dry bread crumbs
½ teaspoon dried basil, crushed
½ teaspoon dried oregano, crushed
½ teaspoon paprika
⅛ teaspoon garlic powder
⅛ teaspoon salt
1 beaten egg or ¼ cup refrigerated or
   frozen egg product, thawed
1½ cups purchased marinara sauce (optional)

● In a medium saucepan cook potatoes, covered, in enough boiling *water* to cover for 20 to 25 minutes or until tender; drain. Mash potatoes; stir in the 1 egg or the ¼ cup egg product. Add the prosciutto or ham, Parmesan or Romano cheese, and fresh basil; mix well.

● Divide the potato mixture into 18 portions and form into balls. Using your finger, make an indentation in each ball. Place a cube of mozzarella cheese in the indentation and mold potato mixture to enclose cheese.

● Combine the bread crumbs, dried basil, oregano, paprika, garlic powder, and salt. Roll each potato ball in the bread crumb mixture. Dip balls into the 1 beaten egg or ¼ cup egg product; roll again in bread crumb mixture. (To serve later, cover and refrigerate the croquettes for up to 24 hours.)

● To serve, place the croquettes on a large lightly greased baking sheet. Bake in a 400° oven for 10 minutes or until heated through (allow about 12 minutes if chilled).

● Meanwhile, if desired, in a small saucepan heat marinara sauce until bubbling. Serve the croquettes warm with marinara sauce. Makes 9 servings.

TOTAL FAT: 4 g
DAILY VALUE FAT: 6%
SATURATED FAT: 2 g
DAILY VALUE SATURATED FAT: 10%

NUTRITION FACTS
PER SERVING:

Calories	136
Total Fat	4 g
Saturated Fat	2 g
Cholesterol	57 mg
Sodium	282 mg
Carbohydrate	16 g
Fiber	1 g
Protein	8 g

EXCHANGES:
1 Starch
1 Lean Meat

PREPARATION TIME: 40 minutes
COOKING TIME: 10 minutes

Polenta with
Tomato-Mushroom Sauce

Asiago cheese is a semifirm Italian cheese that lends a rich nutty flavor to dishes. Look for it in Italian food markets or in the specialty cheese section of your supermarket. Parmesan cheese makes a comparable substitute.

2   **cups water**
¾   **cup cornmeal**
¾   **cup cold water**
¼   **teaspoon salt**
¼   **cup grated Asiago or Parmesan cheese
     (2 ounces)**
1   **recipe Tomato-Mushroom Sauce**

● In a medium saucepan bring the 2 cups water to boiling. Combine the cornmeal, ¾ cup water, and salt. Slowly add cornmeal mixture to the boiling water, stirring constantly. Cook and stir until mixture returns to boiling. Reduce heat to low. Cook, uncovered, for 10 to 15 minutes or until thick, stirring frequently. Stir in the cheese.

● Spread the hot polenta in an ungreased 2-quart square baking dish. Cool polenta slightly. Cover and chill for 30 minutes or until firm. Bake, uncovered, in a 350° oven about 20 minutes or until hot. Cut into 6 rectangles; cut each rectangle in half diagonally to form 12 triangles. Serve immediately with Tomato-Mushroom Sauce. Makes 12 servings.

Tomato-Mushroom Sauce: In a medium saucepan cook 2 cups sliced *fresh mushrooms;* 1 small *onion,* chopped; and 1 clove *garlic,* minced, in 1 tablespoon hot *cooking oil* or *margarine* until tender. Cook and stir on medium-high heat for 10 minutes.

   Meanwhile, place one 16-ounce can *whole Italian-style tomatoes* in a blender container. Cover and blend until smooth. Stir the blended tomatoes and 1 teaspoon *sugar* into the mushroom mixture. Simmer, uncovered, for 15 to 20 minutes or to desired consistency.

   Stir in 1 tablespoon snipped *fresh basil* or 1 teaspoon *dried basil,* crushed; ⅛ teaspoon *salt;* and dash *pepper.* Heat through.

TOTAL FAT: 2 g
DAILY VALUE FAT: 3%
SATURATED FAT: 1 g
DAILY VALUE SATURATED FAT: 5%

NUTRITION FACTS
PER SERVING:

Calories	63
Total Fat	2 g
Saturated Fat	1 g
Cholesterol	2 mg
Sodium	142 mg
Carbohydrate	9 g
Fiber	1 g
Protein	2 g

EXCHANGES:
½ **Starch**
½ **Vegetable**
½ **Fat**

PREPARATION TIME: 30 minutes
CHILLING TIME: 30 minutes
COOKING TIME: 20 minutes

TOTAL FAT: 1 g
DAILY VALUE FAT: 2%
SATURATED FAT: 0%
DAILY VALUE SATURATED FAT: 0%

NUTRITION FACTS
PER SERVING:

Calories	21
Total Fat	1 g
Saturated Fat	0 g
Cholesterol	0 mg
Sodium	37 mg
Carbohydrate	3 g
Fiber	1 g
Protein	0 g

EXCHANGES:
Free Food

PREPARATION TIME: 15 minutes
COOKING TIME: 15 minutes
COOLING TIME: 20 minutes

Caponata

Eggplant stars in this rustic Sicilian appetizer. Serve caponata as a relish or on toasted baguette rounds. Our version uses only 2 teaspoons of oil and saves about 67 calories and 7 grams of fat compared to traditional caponata recipes. (Pictured on page 25, lower right.) A ¼-cup serving is a "free food" exchange.

1 medium onion, sliced and separated into rings
¼ cup sliced celery
2 teaspoons olive oil or cooking oil
1 medium eggplant (1 pound), peeled and cut into ½-inch cubes (about 4 cups)
1 medium yellow summer squash, cut into ½-inch cubes (about 1¼ cups)
1 small tomato, peeled, seeded, and chopped
2 tablespoons halved pimiento-stuffed olives
2 tablespoons red wine vinegar
1 tablespoon capers, rinsed and drained
1 tablespoon raisins (optional)
1 teaspoon sugar
1 tablespoon pine nuts or slivered almonds (optional)

● In a large skillet cook onion and celery in hot oil until tender. Add eggplant, squash, tomato, olives, vinegar, capers, raisins (if desired), and sugar; stir to combine. Simmer mixture, covered, for 8 to 10 minutes or until eggplant and squash are tender. Simmer, uncovered, for 5 to 10 minutes more or until most of the liquid has evaporated. Season to taste with *salt* and *pepper*. Cool slightly. If desired, add pine nuts. Cool and serve at room temperature. (Or, cover and chill overnight. Let stand at room temperature for 20 minutes before serving.) Makes fourteen ¼-cup servings (about 3½ cups).

Lemon-Olive Spread

Open an Italian meal by serving this savory spread as an antipasto—literally meaning "before the pasta."
Our version has no added oil. (Pictured on page 25, lower left.)

½ **cup fresh Italian or French bread crumbs**
1 **cup chopped, pitted ripe olives (about**
   18 to 20 extra-large olives)
½ **teaspoon finely shredded lemon peel**
1 **tablespoon lemon juice**
1 **teaspoon coarse-grain mustard**
1 **clove garlic, minced**
1 **baguette-style French bread**
3 **cherry tomatoes, cut into wedges**
   (optional)
   Fresh oregano (optional)

● Place bread crumbs in a food processor bowl. Cover and process crumbs until very fine. Add the olives, lemon peel, lemon juice, mustard, and garlic; process to a pastelike consistency.

● To serve, cut bread into ½-inch slices. Spread each slice with olive mixture. If desired, top each with a tomato wedge and garnish with fresh oregano. Makes 12 one-tablespoon servings.

The Olive Branch

When first picked, olives have a bitter taste. A curing process removes the bitterness and produces the characteristic flavor. The flavor after processing depends on the ripeness and the type of processing used. Unripe olives are green; ripe olives may be green or black. Although we generally call for ripe pitted olives that are easily found in the canned vegetable section of the supermarket, there are other delicious varieties from which to choose. Greek kalamata and French niçoise olives are popular imported ripe olives. Spanish-style or green olives are underripe olives. The small, shriveled, Italian-style olives are salt-cured and coated with oil.

TOTAL FAT: 1 g
DAILY VALUE FAT: 1%
SATURATED FAT: 0 g
DAILY VALUE SATURATED FAT: 0%

NUTRITION FACTS
PER TABLESPOON:

Calories	15
Total Fat	1 g
Saturated Fat	0 g
Cholesterol	0 mg
Sodium	49 mg
Carbohydrate	1 g
Fiber	0 g
Protein	0 g

EXCHANGES:
Free Food

START TO FINISH: 15 minutes

Fresh Tomato Soup with Tortellini,
recipe on page 35

Spring Vegetable Soup,
recipe on page 34

Soups

Minestrone more than likely comes to mind when you think of an Italian soup. You'll find it included in this collection (with a make-ahead twist), along with many other delicious soup choices. Savor Roasted Garlic Soup with Pesto (page 38), Lentil Soup (page 42), or Pasta and Bean Soup (page 43)—an Italian classic. Most make a hearty meal when served with a salad and a warm loaf of Italian bread.

TOTAL FAT: 3 g
DAILY VALUE FAT: 4%
SATURATED FAT: 1 g
DAILY VALUE SATURATED FAT: 5%

NUTRITION FACTS
PER SIDE-DISH SERVING:

Calories	152
Total Fat	3 g
Saturated Fat	1 g
Cholesterol	4 mg
Sodium	695 mg
Carbohydrate	21 g
Fiber	6 g
Protein	11 g

EXCHANGES:
1 Starch
1 Vegetable
1 Lean Meat

PREPARATION TIME: 30 minutes
COOKING TIME: 20 minutes

Spring Vegetable Soup

Italians classify soups as either zuppa, *a thick soup, or* minestra, *a soup in which the ingredients stand out from the broth. This minestra-style soup plays up asparagus, fava beans, peas, and young artichokes, with a hint of flavor from fresh fennel and pancetta. (Pictured on pages 32 and 33.)*

12 baby artichokes
 6 cups chicken broth or reduced-sodium chicken broth
 1 cup small boiling onions, peeled and halved, or pearl onions
 4 ounces pancetta or 5 slices bacon, crisp-cooked, drained, and cut into small pieces
 1 teaspoon fennel seed, crushed
 ¼ teaspoon pepper
 2 cups cooked* or canned fava or lima beans, rinsed and drained
12 ounces asparagus spears, trimmed and cut into 1-inch pieces
 1 medium fennel bulb, chopped
 ¼ cup snipped fresh fennel leaves

● Remove tough outer green leaves from artichokes (inside leaves will be more tender and greenish yellow). Snip off about 1 inch from the leaf tops, cutting where the green meets the yellow. Trim the stems. Quarter the artichokes lengthwise and set aside.

● In a 4-quart kettle combine broth, onions, pancetta or bacon, fennel seed, and pepper. Bring to boiling; reduce heat. Cover and simmer for 10 minutes. Add the artichokes and beans; cook for 5 minutes. Add the asparagus and chopped fennel; cook for 5 minutes more or until vegetables are tender.

● To serve, ladle into soup bowls. Top with snipped fennel leaves. Makes 8 side-dish servings or 4 main-dish servings.

*Note: To cook fresh or frozen fava or lima beans, simmer, covered, in a small amount of boiling water for 15 to 25 minutes or until tender. Drain and cool slightly. When cool, remove skins from fava beans. For 2 cups of cooked fava beans, purchase 2 pounds of fava beans in the pod.

Fresh Tomato Soup
With Tortellini

Tortellini (tohr-te-LEE-nee)—hat-shaped pasta filled with meat or cheese—is a favorite in Bologna, Italy. (Pictured on page 32.)

1   cup chopped onion
1   tablespoon olive oil or cooking oil
2   pounds ripe tomatoes (about 6 medium), peeled, seeded, and cut up
1½ cups reduced-sodium chicken broth
1½ cups water
1   8-ounce can low-sodium tomato sauce
1   tablespoon snipped fresh sage
    or 1 teaspoon dried sage, crushed
¼ teaspoon salt
¼ teaspoon pepper
4   ounces packaged dried tortellini
¼ cup finely shredded Parmesan cheese
    Fresh sage (optional)

● In a large saucepan cook onion in hot oil until tender. Add tomatoes, broth, water, tomato sauce, sage, salt, and pepper. Bring to boiling; reduce heat. Cover; simmer 30 minutes. Cool.

● Meanwhile, cook tortellini according to package directions; drain. Press tomato mixture through a food mill. (Or, place one-third to one-half of the mixture at a time in a blender container or food processor bowl. Cover and blend or process until smooth.)

● Return mixture to pan. Add drained tortellini; heat through. To serve, ladle into soup bowls; sprinkle with cheese. If desired, garnish with sage. Makes 6 side-dish or 4 main-dish servings.

Sodium Savings

The Dietary Guidelines recommend a daily limit of 2,400 mg of sodium. Here's a comparison of various canned tomato products:

Product	Amount	Sodium (mg)
Tomatoes	½ cup	196
Low-sodium tomatoes	½ cup	16
Tomato sauce	½ cup	741
Low-sodium tomato sauce	½ cup	38
Tomato paste	1 tablespoon	129
Low-sodium tomato paste	1 tablespoon	11

TOTAL FAT: 6 g
DAILY VALUE FAT: 9%
SATURATED FAT: 1 g
DAILY VALUE SATURATED FAT: 5%

NUTRITION FACTS
PER SIDE-DISH SERVING:

Calories	177
Total Fat	6 g
Saturated Fat	1 g
Cholesterol	3 mg
Sodium	496 mg
Carbohydrate	23 g
Fiber	3 g
Protein	8 g

EXCHANGES:
1 Starch
2 Vegetable
1 Fat

PREPARATION TIME: 25 minutes
COOKING TIME: 10 minutes

TOTAL FAT: 2 g
DAILY VALUE FAT: 3%
SATURATED FAT: 0 g
DAILY VALUE SATURATED FAT: 0%

NUTRITION FACTS
PER SERVING:

Calories	214
Total Fat	2 g
Saturated Fat	0 g
Cholesterol	0 mg
Sodium	975 mg
Carbohydrate	41 g
Fiber	9 g
Protein	12 g

EXCHANGES:

2 Starch
1 Vegetable
1 Very Lean Meat

PREPARATION TIME: 15 minutes
COOKING TIME: 10 minutes

Make-Ahead Minestrone

You can serve this meatless soup immediately, but chilling the soup overnight allows the flavors to blend. If you like, serve it country-style over thick slices of toasted Italian bread.

3 14½-ounce cans beef broth
1 15-ounce can kidney beans, rinsed and drained
1 15-ounce can garbanzo beans, rinsed and drained
1 14½-ounce can low-sodium stewed tomatoes
1 11½-ounce can vegetable juice
1 6-ounce can low-sodium tomato paste
2 teaspoons sugar
1 teaspoon dried Italian seasoning, crushed
1½ cups loose-pack frozen mixed vegetables (such as an Italian blend)
2 cups fresh spinach leaves, cut in strips
2 cups cooked pasta (1 cup uncooked), such as small shells or mostaccioli
   Finely shredded Parmesan cheese (optional)

● In a large kettle combine broth, beans, stewed tomatoes, vegetable juice, tomato paste, sugar, and Italian seasoning. Bring to boiling. Add mixed vegetables. Reduce heat. Cover and simmer about 10 minutes or until vegetables are tender. Remove from heat; cool. Refrigerate, covered, overnight. (Or, to serve immediately, add spinach and cooked pasta; heat through.)

● To serve, reheat soup over medium heat. Stir in spinach and cooked pasta. Heat through. To serve, ladle into bowls. If desired, sprinkle with Parmesan cheese. Makes 8 main-dish servings.

Note: If you're concerned about your sodium intake, use two 15½-ounce cans reduced-sodium dark red kidney beans in place of the regular kidney beans and garbanzo beans, and 1½ cups of no salt added vegetable juice in place of the 11½-ounce can vegetable juice.

Full of Beans

Fat-smart cooks know to look for recipes that are full of beans. Unlike other high-protein sources, such as meat and cheese, beans contain almost no saturated fat and no cholesterol. In addition, they're high in fiber. Canned beans are a convenient alternative to dried beans because they require no soaking or cooking. However, they are high in sodium. Before adding canned beans to a dish, place them in a colander and rinse with cold water. Rinsing helps to remove some of the sodium.

TOTAL FAT: 6 g
DAILY VALUE FAT: 9%
SATURATED FAT: 1 g
DAILY VALUE SATURATED FAT: 5%

NUTRITION FACTS
PER SERVING:

Calories	190
Total Fat	6 g
Saturated Fat	1 g
Cholesterol	5 mg
Sodium	652 mg
Carbohydrate	27 g
Fiber	2 g
Protein	9 g

EXCHANGES:
1 Starch
1 Vegetable
½ Milk
1 Fat

PREPARATION TIME: 35 minutes
COOKING TIME: 11 minutes

Roasted Garlic Soup with Pesto

While the garlic roasts in the oven, make the pesto. Or, even better, make the pesto ahead of time.

- 2 **heads garlic**
- ½ **teaspoon olive oil**
- 1 **medium potato, peeled and cubed**
- 2 **medium leeks, chopped (⅔ cup)**
- ½ **cup chopped onion**
- ⅓ **cup water**
- 2 **teaspoons instant chicken bouillon granules**
- ¼ **teaspoon pepper**
- 2 **cups skim milk**
- 2 **tablespoons all-purpose flour**
- 4 **to 6 tablespoons Pesto**

● For garlic, peel away the dry outer layers of skin from the garlic heads. Leave skins of cloves intact. Cut off the pointed top portion (about ¼ inch) with a knife, leaving the bulb intact but exposing the individual cloves.

● Place garlic, cut side up, in a small baking dish. Brush sides and top of garlic with olive oil. Bake, covered, in a 400° oven for 25 to 35 minutes or until cloves feel soft when pressed. When cool enough to handle, press the garlic paste from the individual cloves (you should have 2 tablespoons).

● In a large saucepan combine the garlic paste, potato, leeks, onion, water, bouillon granules, and pepper. Bring to boiling; reduce heat. Cover and simmer about 10 minutes or until potato is tender, stirring occasionally. Stir in *1½ cups* of the milk. Gradually stir the remaining milk into the flour; stir into the mixture in the saucepan. Cook and stir until thickened and bubbly. Cook and stir 1 minute more.

● To serve, ladle into soup bowls. Top each serving with about 1 tablespoon of Pesto; swirl slightly with a knife. (If necessary, thin Pesto with a small amount of water before using.) Makes 4 to 6 side-dish servings.

Pesto: In a blender container or food processor bowl combine 1 cup firmly packed *fresh basil leaves,* ½ cup torn *fresh spinach leaves,* ¼ cup grated *Parmesan* or *Romano cheese,* ¼ cup *pine nuts* or *almonds,* ¼ teaspoon *salt,* and 2 cloves *garlic,* quartered. Cover; blend or process with several on-off turns until a paste forms, stopping the machine several times and scraping the sides. With the machine running slowly, gradually add 2 tablespoons *olive oil* and 2 tablespoons *water;* blend or process until mixture is the consistency of soft butter. Transfer to a storage container. Cover and refrigerate for up to 2 days or freeze for up to 1 month. Makes ½ cup.

Lamb and Orzo Soup
With Spinach

Orzo, also called rosamarina, is a tiny pasta shaped like long grains of rice.

2½ **pounds lamb shanks**
4 **cups water**
4 **cups reduced-sodium chicken broth or**
    vegetable broth
2 **bay leaves**
1 **tablespoon snipped fresh oregano**
    or 1 teaspoon dried oregano, crushed
1½ **teaspoons snipped fresh marjoram or**
    ½ **teaspoon dried marjoram, crushed**
¼ **teaspoon pepper**
2 **carrots, cut into short thin strips**
1 **cup sliced celery**
¾ **cup packaged dried orzo (rosamarina)**
3 **cups torn fresh spinach or** ½ **of a**
    10-ounce package frozen chopped
    spinach, thawed and well drained
    Finely shredded Parmesan cheese
    (optional)

● In a large kettle combine shanks, water, broth, bay leaves, oregano, marjoram, and pepper. Bring to boiling. Reduce heat and simmer, covered, for 1¼ to 1½ hours or until meat is tender.

● Remove meat from soup; set aside to cool. Strain broth through a large sieve or colander lined with 2 layers of 100-percent-cotton cheesecloth; discard herbs. Skim fat; return broth to kettle. Cut meat off bones and coarsely chop meat; discard bones.

● Stir meat, carrots, celery, and orzo into soup. Return to boiling; reduce heat. Cover; simmer 15 minutes or until vegetables and orzo are tender. Stir in spinach. Cook for 1 to 2 minutes more or just until spinach wilts. Ladle into soup bowls. If desired, sprinkle with cheese. Serves 6.

Broth Options

Broth-based soups are low in fat but can wreak havoc with your sodium intake. If you are concerned about sodium, choose low-sodium chicken broth. Compare these products based on 1 cup broth:

Low-sodium broth	54 mg
Regular broth	776 mg
1 bouillon cube	1,152 mg
(makes 1 cup broth)	

TOTAL FAT: 3 g
DAILY VALUE FAT: 4%
SATURATED FAT: 1 g
DAILY VALUE SATURATED FAT: 5%

NUTRITION FACTS
PER SERVING:

Calories	161
Total Fat	3 g
Saturated Fat	1 g
Cholesterol	45 mg
Sodium	462 mg
Carbohydrate	15 g
Fiber	2 g
Protein	18 g

EXCHANGES:
½ **Starch**
1½ **Vegetable**
2 **Lean Meat**

PREPARATION TIME: 15 minutes
COOKING TIME: 1 hour and
50 minutes

Meatball Soup

This meal in a bowl features mini-meatballs made with lean ground beef. It was created to resemble "wedding soup," which is found in some Italian restaurants in America.

1 beaten egg
½ cup soft bread crumbs
2 tablespoons grated Parmesan or Romano cheese
1 tablespoon snipped parsley
1 tablespoon finely chopped onion
¼ teaspoon garlic powder
⅛ teaspoon ground red pepper
8 ounces lean ground beef
   Nonstick spray coating
2 cups water
1 15-ounce can garbanzo beans, drained
1 14½-ounce can beef broth
1 14½-ounce can low-sodium stewed tomatoes
1 9-ounce package frozen Italian green beans
1 cup sliced fresh mushrooms
1½ teaspoons dried Italian seasoning, crushed
½ teaspoon fennel seed, crushed (optional)

● In a medium bowl combine egg, bread crumbs, Parmesan or Romano cheese, parsley, onion, garlic powder, and red pepper. Add the ground beef; mix well. Shape the mixture into 36 balls.

● Spray a 2-quart square baking dish with nonstick coating. Place the meatballs in the dish. Bake, uncovered, in a 375° oven for 15 to 20 minutes or until juices run clear. Drain well. Set meatballs aside.

● Meanwhile, in a large saucepan stir together the water, garbanzo beans, beef broth, *undrained* tomatoes, Italian green beans, mushrooms, Italian seasoning, and, if desired, fennel seed. Bring mixture to boiling; reduce heat. Cover and simmer for 10 minutes. Stir in the meatballs; heat through. To serve, ladle into soup bowls. Makes 6 main-dish servings.

TOTAL FAT: 7 g
DAILY VALUE FAT: 10%
SATURATED FAT: 3 g
DAILY VALUE SATURATED FAT: 15%

NUTRITION FACTS PER SERVING:

Calories	211
Total Fat	7 g
Saturated Fat	3 g
Cholesterol	64 mg
Sodium	438 mg
Carbohydrate	22 g
Fiber	5 g
Protein	16 g

EXCHANGES:
1 Starch
2 Vegetable
1 Lean Meat
½ Fat

START TO FINISH: 45 minutes

**NUTRITION FACTS
PER SERVING:**

Calories	180
Total Fat	3 g
Saturated Fat	1 g
Cholesterol	4 mg
Sodium	546 mg
Carbohydrate	26 g
Fiber	6 g
Protein	13 g

EXCHANGES:
1½ Starch
1½ Very Lean Meat

**PREPARATION TIME: 10 minutes
COOKING TIME: 35 minutes**

Lentil Soup

Lentils are a symbol of wealth and prosperity in Italy and are a must at that country's New Year dinner table. This version contains less oil and pancetta, or Italian-style bacon.

1   cup dry lentils
4   cups water
2   ounces pancetta or 3 slices bacon,
      crisp-cooked and crumbled
2   teaspoons beef bouillon granules
2   tablespoons snipped fresh basil or
      1 teaspoon dried basil, crushed
1   tablespoon snipped fresh marjoram or
      ½ teaspoon dried marjoram, crushed
1   tablespoon low-sodium tomato paste
2   bay leaves
4   thick slices baguette-style French bread,
      toasted (optional)
¼   cup finely shredded Parmesan cheese
      (optional)

● Rinse lentils. In a large saucepan combine water, crumbled pancetta or bacon, bouillon granules, basil, marjoram, tomato paste, and bay leaves. Bring to boiling; reduce heat. Cover and simmer for 30 minutes or until lentils are tender. Discard bay leaves. If desired, sprinkle toasted bread with cheese. Place bread under broiler until cheese melts.

● To serve, ladle into soup bowls. If desired, top each serving with a slice of toasted bread. Makes 4 main-dish servings.

Ladle on the Lentils

Whether or not lentils really bring wealth and prosperity, as folklore suggests above, is open for debate, but one thing is for sure: Lentils are an excellent source of protein. They also supply fiber, calcium, vitamin B, iron, and phosphorous to your diet. With a beanlike texture and a mild, nutty flavor, they're an excellent addition to soups as well as salads, casseroles, and stews.

Pasta and Bean Soup

It is traditional to drizzle a little olive oil into the soup when it is served, but it's not a must. Olive oil will, however, add a wonderful flavor to the soup.

⅔ cup dried cannellini beans or navy beans
4 cups water to soak beans
5 cups water
½ cup chopped onion
½ cup chopped carrot
¼ cup chopped celery
1 ounce pancetta or 2 slices bacon, crisp-cooked and crumbled
1 tablespoon instant beef bouillon granules
2 cloves garlic, minced
½ teaspoon dried sage, crushed
½ teaspoon dried marjoram, crushed
⅛ teaspoon pepper
½ cup packaged dried small pasta (such as shells, elbow macaroni, or bow ties)
4 teaspoons olive oil (optional)

● Rinse beans. In a large saucepan combine beans and 4 cups water. Bring to boiling; reduce heat and simmer for 2 minutes. Remove from heat. Cover and let stand for 1 hour. (Or, skip boiling the water and soak beans overnight in a covered pan.)

● Drain and rinse the soaked beans. In the same pan combine beans, the 5 cups fresh water, onion, carrot, celery, crumbled pancetta or bacon, bouillon granules, garlic, sage, marjoram, and pepper. Bring to boiling; reduce heat. Cover and simmer for 1 to 1½ hours or until beans are tender.* Slightly mash beans in saucepan. Stir in *uncooked* pasta. Increase heat and boil gently, uncovered, for 8 to 10 minutes or just until pasta is tender. To serve, ladle into soup bowls. If desired, drizzle each serving with 1 teaspoon olive oil. Makes 4 main-dish servings.

Shortcut Pasta and Bean Soup: Prepare soup as directed above, *except* omit dry beans and their soaking step. In a large saucepan combine 3½ cups *water,* the onion, carrot, celery, pancetta or bacon, bouillon granules, garlic, sage, marjoram, and pepper. Bring to boiling; reduce heat. Cover and simmer for 15 minutes or until vegetables are tender. Stir in one 15-ounce can *cannellini* or *navy beans,* rinsed and drained. Continue as directed following the asterisk (*).

TOTAL FAT: 2 g
DAILY VALUE FAT: 3%
SATURATED FAT: 1 g
DAILY VALUE SATURATED FAT: 5%

NUTRITION FACTS PER SERVING:

Calories	183
Total Fat	2 g
Saturated Fat	1 g
Cholesterol	3 mg
Sodium	770 mg
Carbohydrate	31 g
Fiber	7 g
Protein	9 g

EXCHANGES:
1½ Starch
1½ Vegetable
½ Lean Meat

PREPARATION TIME: 1⅓ hours
COOKING TIME: 1 hour and 10 minutes

TOTAL FAT: 3 g
DAILY VALUE FAT: 4%
SATURATED FAT: 0 g
DAILY VALUE SATURATED FAT: 0%

**NUTRITION FACTS
PER SERVING:**

Calories	252
Total Fat	3 g
Saturated Fat	0 g
Cholesterol	96 mg
Sodium	780 mg
Carbohydrate	30 g
Fiber	5 g
Protein	24 g

EXCHANGES:
1½ Starch
2 Vegetable
2 Very Lean Meat

PREPARATION TIME: 20 minutes
COOKING TIME: 25 minutes

Italian Fish Soup

In Italy, there are as many versions of zuppa di pesce, *or fish soup, as there are coastal towns. Serve fish soup as the Italians do—topped with a slice of toasted Italian bread.*

8 ounces fresh or frozen haddock, bass, sole, or other fish fillets
6 ounces fresh or frozen peeled and deveined shrimp
3 cups water
2 medium tomatoes, peeled and cut up
½ cup dry white wine or water
1 cup thinly sliced carrots (2 medium)
½ cup chopped celery (2 stalks)
⅓ cup chopped onion
2 teaspoons instant chicken bouillon granules
½ teaspoon dried marjoram, crushed
½ teaspoon shredded orange peel
2 cloves garlic, minced
2 bay leaves
   Dash bottled hot pepper sauce
¼ cup tomato paste
4 slices Italian bread, toasted

● Thaw the fish fillets and shrimp, if frozen. Cut the fish into 1-inch pieces; halve shrimp lengthwise. Chill.

● In a large saucepan combine the 3 cups water, the tomatoes, wine or water, carrots, celery, onion, bouillon granules, marjoram, orange peel, garlic, bay leaves, and hot pepper sauce. Bring to boiling; reduce heat. Cover and simmer for 15 to 20 minutes or until vegetables are nearly tender. Stir in tomato paste.

● Add fish pieces and shrimp to saucepan. Bring mixture just to boiling. Reduce heat. Cover and simmer about 5 minutes more or until fish flakes easily when tested with a fork and shrimp turn pink. Discard bay leaves.

● To serve, ladle into soup bowls. Place a slice of Italian bread on each serving. Serve immediately. Makes 4 main-dish servings.

Whole Wheat Pesto Pizza, recipe on page 62

Buccellato,
recipe on page 48

Breads, Pizza, Etc.

Italian cooks definitely know how to bake bread, and their skill is equalled only by their diversity of mouthwatering breads. In this chapter, we've included not only breads but pizza and sandwiches, too. Look for Calzones (page 67), the Italian-style turnover; Pizza Rustica (page 60); Easy Herb Focaccia (page 54); Pepper and Fennel Batter Bread (page 53); Spicy Italian "Sausage" Sandwich (page 70); and Tomato Polenta Pizza (page 68). We've also included a special page of tips on converting the bread recipes from a conventional method to using a bread machine (page 59).

TOTAL FAT: 3 g
DAILY VALUE FAT: 4%
SATURATED FAT: 1 g
DAILY VALUE SATURATED FAT: 5%

NUTRITION FACTS
PER SERVING:

Calories	150
Total Fat	3 g
Saturated Fat	1 g
Cholesterol	40 mg
Sodium	100 mg
Carbohydrate	26 g
Fiber	1 g
Protein	4 g

EXCHANGES:
1 Starch
½ Fruit
½ Fat

PREPARATION TIME: 20 minutes
RISING TIMES: 1¼ hours; 45 minutes
RESTING TIME: 10 minutes
BAKING TIME: 40 minutes

Buccellato

Buccellato (book-chahl-LAH-toa) is a sweet bread that originated in the town of Lucca, Italy. Serve it with fresh fruit as a dessert or as a snack. (Pictured on pages 46 and 47.)

2¾ to 3¼ cups all-purpose flour
  1 package active dry yeast
  ¼ cup skim milk
  ¼ cup honey
  3 tablespoons margarine or butter
  ½ teaspoon salt
  2 eggs
  ¼ cup dry or sweet marsala or skim milk
  ⅓ cup chopped mixed candied fruits and
    peels
  ¼ cup golden raisins
1½ teaspoons aniseed, crushed
  1 teaspoon finely shredded orange peel
  1 slightly beaten egg
  1 tablespoon water

● In a large mixing bowl combine *1 cup* of the flour and the yeast. In a small saucepan heat and stir the ¼ cup milk, the honey, margarine or butter, and salt just until warm (120° to 130°) and margarine almost melts. Add to flour mixture; add the 2 eggs and the marsala or milk. Beat with an electric mixer on low speed for 30 seconds, scraping bowl. Beat on high speed for 3 minutes. Stir in candied fruits and peels, raisins, aniseed, and orange peel. Using a wooden spoon, stir in as much of the remaining flour as you can.

● On a floured surface, knead in enough of the remaining flour to make a moderately soft dough that is smooth and elastic (3 to 5 minutes total). Place dough in greased bowl; turn once to grease the surface. Cover and let rise in a warm place until double (1¼ to 1½ hours).

● Punch dough down. Cover and let rest for 10 minutes. Shape into a ball. Place on a greased baking sheet. Flatten into an 8-inch round. Cut a cross, ½ inch deep, in top. Cover; let rise until nearly double (about 45 minutes). Brush with mixture of the 1 beaten egg and water. Bake in a 325° oven about 40 to 45 minutes or until golden. (If necessary, cover loaf with foil during the last 15 to 20 minutes of baking to prevent overbrowning.) Cool on a wire rack. Makes 1 loaf (16 servings).

Italian Bread

One bite of this classic Italian bread and you'll be glad that bread fits quite nicely into a healthful eating plan. For a special treat, drizzle this fresh-from-the-oven bread with a touch of fruity olive oil.

5½ **to 6 cups all-purpose flour**
 2 **packages active dry yeast**
1½ **teaspoons salt**
 2 **cups warm water (120° to 130°)**
    Cornmeal
 1 **slightly beaten egg white**
 1 **tablespoon water**
¼ **teaspoon dried rosemary or basil, crushed, or ⅛ teaspoon onion powder or garlic powder (optional)**

● In a large mixing bowl combine *2 cups* of the flour, the yeast, and salt. Add the 2 cups warm water. Beat with an electric mixer on low speed for 30 seconds, scraping bowl. Beat on high speed for 3 minutes. Using a wooden spoon stir in as much of the remaining flour as you can.

● On a floured surface, knead in enough remaining flour to make a stiff dough that is smooth and elastic (8 to 10 minutes total). Shape into a ball. Place dough in a greased bowl; turn once to grease surface. Cover and let rise in a warm place until double (1 to 1½ hours).

● Punch dough down. Divide in half. Cover; let rest 10 minutes. Grease 2 baking sheets; sprinkle with cornmeal. On a lightly floured surface, roll each dough half into a 15×12-inch rectangle. Roll up from long side; seal well. Taper ends.

● Place, seam side down, on prepared baking sheets. Brush with a mixture of egg white, the 1 tablespoon water, and, if desired, an herb or onion or garlic powder. Cover and let rise until nearly double (about 45 minutes). Make 5 or 6 diagonal cuts, ¼ inch deep, across tops.

● Bake in a 375° oven for 20 minutes. Brush again with the egg white mixture. Bake 20 to 25 minutes more or until bread sounds hollow when tapped. Cool on a wire rack. Makes 2 loaves (30 servings).

Breadsticks: Prepare Italian Bread as above, *except* divide each half of dough into 15 pieces. Roll each piece into an 8-inch rope. Place ropes on prepared baking sheets. Cover and let rise until nearly double (about 30 minutes). Brush with the egg white mixture. Bake in a 375° oven for 10 minutes. Brush again with egg white mixture. Reduce oven temperature to 300° and bake for 20 to 25 minutes more or until golden. Cool. Makes 30 breadsticks.

TOTAL FAT: 0 g
DAILY VALUE FAT: 0%
SATURATED FAT: 0 g
DAILY VALUE SATURATED FAT: 0%

NUTRITION FACTS PER SERVING:

Calories	80
Total Fat	0 g
Saturated Fat	0 g
Cholesterol	0 mg
Sodium	109 mg
Carbohydrate	17 g
Fiber	1 g
Protein	3 g

EXCHANGES:
1 Starch

PREPARATION TIME: 15 minutes
RISING TIMES: 1 hour; 45 minutes
RESTING TIME: 10 minutes
BAKING TIME: 40 minutes

TOTAL FAT: 1 g
DAILY VALUE FAT: 1%
SATURATED FAT: 0 g
DAILY VALUE SATURATED FAT: 0%

NUTRITION FACTS
PER SERVING:

Calories	102
Total Fat	1 g
Saturated Fat	0 g
Cholesterol	0 mg
Sodium	111 mg
Carbohydrate	19 g
Fiber	1 g
Protein	3 g

EXCHANGES:
1½ Starch

PREPARATION TIME: 30 minutes
RISING TIMES: 1 hour; 30 minutes
RESTING TIME: 10 minutes
BAKING TIME: 30 minutes

Pine Nut Bread

Toasting the nuts brings out their rich flavor so you can use fewer of them. Cracked wheat also adds a nutty, crunchy texture.

 ½ **cup boiling water**
 ¼ **cup cracked wheat**
2½ **to 3 cups all-purpose flour**
 1 **package active dry yeast**
 ¾ **teaspoon salt**
 ½ **cup warm water (120° to 130°)**
 2 **teaspoons olive oil or cooking oil**
 ¼ **cup pine nuts or sunflower nuts, toasted
     and coarsely chopped**
    Cornmeal
 1 **slightly beaten egg white**
 1 **tablespoon water**

● Pour the boiling water over the cracked wheat. Let stand about 20 minutes or until most of the liquid is absorbed. *Do not drain.* Set aside.

● Meanwhile, in a medium mixing bowl stir together *¾ cup* of the flour, the yeast, and the salt. Add the warm water and oil. Beat with an electric mixer on low speed for 30 seconds, scraping bowl. Beat on high speed for 3 minutes. Using a wooden spoon, stir in the *undrained* cracked wheat and pine nuts. Stir in as much of the remaining flour as you can.

● On a lightly floured surface, knead in enough of the remaining flour to make a stiff dough that is smooth and elastic (8 to 10 minutes total).

Shape into a ball. Place in a lightly greased bowl; turn once to grease surface. Cover and let rise in a warm place until double (about 1 hour).

● Punch dough down. Cover and let rest for 10 minutes. Grease a baking sheet and sprinkle with cornmeal. On a lightly floured surface, roll the dough into a 15×11-inch rectangle. Roll up tightly from long side; seal well. Taper ends. Place, seam side down, on prepared baking sheet. Brush with a mixture of egg white and the 1 tablespoon water. Cover and let rise until nearly double (about 30 minutes).

● Using a sharp knife, make 3 or 4 diagonal cuts about ¼-inch deep across the top of the loaf. Bake in a 375° oven for 20 minutes. Brush again with the egg white mixture. Bake 10 to 15 minutes more or until bread sounds hollow when tapped. Cool on wire rack. Makes 1 loaf (15 servings).

Olive Bread: Prepare Pine Nut Bread as above *except* substitute ¼ cup sliced *pitted ripe olives* for the pine nuts or sunflower nuts.

Note: This recipe may be doubled.

Polenta Bread

You can substitute fine-ground cornmeal for the quick-cooking polenta called for in this recipe.

2¼ to 2¾ cups all-purpose flour
1 package active dry yeast
1 cup milk
2 tablespoons packed brown sugar
2 tablespoons olive oil
1 teaspoon salt
¼ cup quick-cooking polenta
   Quick-cooking polenta
1 slightly beaten egg white
1 tablespoon water
   Fresh sage sprigs (optional)

● In a mixing bowl stir together *1 cup* of the flour and the yeast. In a saucepan heat the milk, brown sugar, oil, and salt until warm (120° to 130°). Add to flour mixture.

● Beat the flour mixture with an electric mixer on low speed for 30 seconds. Beat on high speed for 3 minutes. Using a wooden spoon, stir in the ¼ cup polenta and as much of the remaining flour as you can.

● On a floured surface, knead in enough of the remaining flour to make a moderately stiff dough that is smooth and elastic (about 8 minutes total). Shape into a ball. Place in a greased bowl; turn once to grease surface. Cover and let rise in a warm place until double (about 1 hour). Punch dough down. Cover; let rest for 10 minutes.

● Grease a baking sheet. Sprinkle with additional polenta. Shape dough into a ball. Place on prepared baking sheet. Flatten to about 5 inches in diameter. Brush loaf with a mixture of the egg white and water. If desired, place sage sprigs on top of loaf or use an extremely sharp knife to make slashes ½-inch deep across the top. Cover and let rise until nearly double (30 to 45 minutes).

● Brush again with egg white mixture. Bake in a 375° oven for 30 to 35 minutes or until bread sounds hollow when tapped. (If necessary, cover with foil the last 15 minutes of baking to prevent overbrowning.) Cool on a wire rack. Makes 1 loaf (14 servings).

Polenta Tomato Bread: Prepare Polenta Bread as above *except* place ¼ cup *dried tomatoes* in a small bowl and cover with *boiling water.* Let stand about 10 minutes. Drain. When cool enough to handle, snip into small pieces. Stir the snipped tomatoes into the batter with the ¼ cup polenta.

TOTAL FAT: 2 g
DAILY VALUE FAT: 3%
SATURATED FAT: 0 g
DAILY VALUE SATURATED FAT: 0%

NUTRITION FACTS PER SERVING:

Calories	124
Total Fat	2 g
Saturated Fat	0 g
Cholesterol	1 mg
Sodium	166 mg
Carbohydrate	22 g
Fiber	1 g
Protein	3 g

EXCHANGES:
1½ Starch

PREPARATION TIME: 20 minutes
RISING TIMES: 1 hour; 30 minutes
RESTING TIME: 10 minutes
BAKING TIME: 30 minutes

Pepper and Fennel
Batter Bread

This batter bread needs only one rising time and saves on elbow grease because there's no kneading required. For maximum pepper flavor, use fresh ground peppercorns. (Pictured at top left of photo.)

2   **cups all-purpose flour**
1   **package active dry yeast**
½   **cup cream-style cottage cheese**
½   **cup water**
1   **tablespoon sugar**
1   **to 1½ teaspoons coarsely ground**
    black pepper
1   **to 2 teaspoons fennel seed, crushed**
1   **tablespoon margarine or butter**
1   **teaspoon dried minced onion**
½   **teaspoon salt**
1   **egg**
½   **cup toasted wheat germ**

● Combine *1 cup* of the flour and the yeast. Heat and stir cottage cheese, water, sugar, black pepper, fennel seed, margarine or butter, onion, and salt until warm (120° to 130°) and margarine almost melts. Add to flour mixture along with egg. Beat with an electric mixer on low speed for 30 seconds, scraping bowl constantly. Beat on high speed for 3 minutes.

● Using a wooden spoon, stir in wheat germ and remaining flour (batter will be stiff). Spoon batter into a well-greased 1-quart casserole or a 9×1½-inch round baking pan. Cover and let rise in a warm place until nearly double (50 to 60 minutes).

● Bake in a 375° oven for 25 to 30 minutes or until bread sounds hollow when lightly tapped. (If necessary, cover with foil during the last 10 minutes of baking to prevent overbrowning.) Remove from casserole or pan. Cool on wire rack. Makes 1 loaf (8 servings).

From top left: Pepper and Fennel Batter Bread *(recipe above)* and Easy Herb Focaccia *(recipe on page 54).*

TOTAL FAT: 4 g
DAILY VALUE FAT: 6%
SATURATED FAT: 1 g
DAILY VALUE SATURATED FAT: 5%

NUTRITION FACTS
PER SERVING:

Calories	187
Total Fat	4 g
Saturated Fat	1 g
Cholesterol	29 mg
Sodium	208 mg
Carbohydrate	30 g
Fiber	2 g
Protein	8 g

EXCHANGES:
2 Starch
1 Fat

PREPARATION TIME: 15 minutes
RISING TIME: 50 minutes
BAKING TIME: 25 minutes

TOTAL FAT: 2 g
DAILY VALUE FAT: 3%
SATURATED FAT: 0 g
DAILY VALUE SATURATED FAT: 0%

NUTRITION FACTS
PER SERVING:

Calories	85
Total Fat	2 g
Saturated Fat	0 g
Cholesterol	9 mg
Sodium	133 mg
Carbohydrate	14 g
Fiber	0 g
Protein	2 g

EXCHANGES:
1 Starch

PREPARATION TIME: 20 minutes
RISING TIME: 30 minutes
BAKING TIME: 15 minutes

Easy Herb Focaccia

Focaccia (foh-COT-see-uh) is an Italian yeast bread usually topped with onions, herbs, olives, or cheese. Our easy version is made with hot roll mix. Serve focaccia warm with pasta or as a snack. (Pictured on page 52 in foreground and upper right of photo.)

1　**16-ounce package hot roll mix**
1　**egg**
2　**tablespoons olive oil**
⅔　**cup finely chopped onion**
1　**teaspoon dried rosemary, crushed**
2　**teaspoons olive oil**

● Lightly grease a 15×10×1-inch baking pan, a 12- to 14-inch pizza pan, or two 9×1½-inch round baking pans. Set aside.

● Prepare the hot roll mix according to package directions for basic dough, using the 1 egg and substituting the 2 tablespoons oil for the margarine. Knead dough; allow to rest as directed. If using large baking pan, roll dough into a 15×10-inch rectangle and carefully transfer to prepared pan. If using a pizza pan, roll dough into a 12-inch round. If using round baking pans, divide dough in half; roll into two 9-inch rounds. Place in prepared pan(s).

● In a skillet cook onion and rosemary in the 2 teaspoons hot oil until tender. With fingertips, press indentations every inch or so in dough round(s). Top dough evenly with onion mixture. Cover; let rise in a warm place until nearly double (about 30 minutes).

● Bake in a 375° oven for 15 to 20 minutes or until golden. Cool 10 minutes on a wire rack(s). Remove from pan(s) and cool completely. Makes 24 servings.

Onion and Sage Focaccia: Prepare Focaccia as above, *except* omit rosemary. Add 3 tablespoons snipped *fresh sage,* 1 tablespoon *dry white wine,* and ¼ teaspoon *pepper* to the dough along with the 2 tablespoons olive oil. Continue as directed.

Lemon and Savory Focaccia: Prepare Focaccia as above, *except* omit the onion, rosemary, and the 2 teaspoons olive oil. Add ¼ cup coarsely chopped pitted *ripe olives,* 3 tablespoons snipped *fresh savory,* and 1 teaspoon finely shredded *lemon peel* to the dough along with the 2 tablespoons olive oil. Continue as directed.

Parmesan and Pine Nut Focaccia: Prepare Focaccia as above, *except* omit the onion, rosemary, and 2 teaspoons olive oil. After making indentations, brush dough with mixture of 1 *egg white* and 1 tablespoon *water.* Sprinkle with ¼ cup *pine nuts,* pressing lightly into dough. Sprinkle with 2 tablespoons fresh grated *Parmesan cheese.* Bake as directed.

Sausage Whole Wheat Bread

This festive bread is perfect party fare. Your guests will never believe it has only 5 grams of fat per serving. For a light meal, serve it with a salad.

  8 **ounces Italian turkey sausage**
  ½ **cup chopped red sweet pepper**
  ¼ **cup chopped onion**
  ½ **of an 8-ounce container fat-free cream cheese**
  ½ **of a 10-ounce package frozen chopped spinach, thawed and well drained**
  1 **16-ounce loaf frozen whole wheat or white bread dough, thawed**
     Pizza sauce (optional)

● For filling, in a 10-inch skillet cook sausage, sweet pepper, and onion until sausage is brown and onion is tender. Remove from heat. Drain well. Stir in cream cheese until melted. Stir in spinach. Set aside.

● On a lightly floured surface, roll dough into a 12×9-inch rectangle. Carefully transfer to a greased baking sheet. Spread filling lengthwise in a 3-inch-wide strip down the center of rectangle to within 1 inch of the ends.

● On both long sides, make 3-inch cuts from the edges toward the center at 1-inch intervals. Moisten the end of each dough strip (this will help to seal the dough when overlapped). Starting at an end, alternately fold opposite strips of dough at an angle across filling. Slightly press moistened ends together in center to seal. Cover and let rise in a warm place until nearly double (about 30 minutes).

● Bake in a 350° oven for 25 to 30 minutes or until golden brown. Cool slightly on a wire rack before cutting. If desired, serve with warm pizza sauce. Cover and refrigerate any leftovers. Makes 10 to 12 servings.

TOTAL FAT: 5 g
DAILY VALUE FAT: 7%
SATURATED FAT: 1 g
DAILY VALUE SATURATED FAT: 5%

**NUTRITION FACTS
PER SERVING:**

Calories	178
Total Fat	5 g
Saturated Fat	1 g
Cholesterol	10 mg
Sodium	435 mg
Carbohydrate	24 g
Fiber	2 g
Protein	12 g

EXCHANGES:
1½ Starch
½ Vegetable
1 Medium-Fat Meat

PREPARATION TIME: 20 minutes
RISING TIME: 30 minutes
COOKING TIME: 25 minutes

Pepper-Cheese Bread

To boost fiber, you can replace up to half of the all-purpose flour with whole wheat flour. The loaf will be denser and coarser in texture.

2¾ to 3¼ cups all-purpose flour
1 package active dry yeast
1½ to 2 teaspoons cracked black pepper
½ teaspoon salt
1 cup warm water (120° to 130°)
2 tablespoons olive oil or cooking oil
½ cup shredded provolone cheese
  (2 ounces)
¼ grated Parmesan or Romano cheese
  (1 ounce)
1 slightly beaten egg white
1 tablespoon water

● In a large mixing bowl stir together *1 cup* of the flour, the yeast, pepper, and salt. Add 1 cup warm water and oil. Beat with an electric mixer on low to medium speed for 30 seconds, scraping the sides of the bowl. Beat on high speed for 3 minutes. Using a wooden spoon, stir in as much of the remaining flour as you can.

● On a lightly floured surface, knead in enough of the remaining flour to make a stiff dough that is smooth and elastic (8 to 10 minutes total). Shape into a ball. Place in a greased bowl; turn once to grease surface. Cover and let rise in a warm place until double (1 to 1¼ hours).

● Punch dough down. Turn out onto a lightly floured surface. Cover and let rest 10 minutes. Meanwhile, lightly grease a large baking sheet. Roll the dough into a 12×10-inch rectangle. Sprinkle provolone cheese and Parmesan or Romano cheese on top of dough. Roll up, jelly-roll style, starting from a long side. Moisten edge with water and seal. Taper ends. Place, seam side down, on prepared baking sheet. Cover and let rise until nearly double (30 to 45 minutes).

● With a sharp knife, make 3 or 4 diagonal cuts about ¼ inch deep across the top of the loaf. Brush the loaf with a mixture of the egg white and 1 tablespoon water. Bake in a 375° oven for 15 minutes. Brush again with egg white mixture. Bake for 20 to 25 minutes more or until loaf sounds hollow when tapped. Remove from baking sheet and cool on a wire rack. Makes 1 loaf (16 servings).

TOTAL FAT: 3 g
DAILY VALUE FAT: 4%
SATURATED FAT: 1 g
DAILY VALUE SATURATED FAT: 5%

NUTRITION FACTS
PER SERVING:

Calories	118
Total Fat	3 g
Saturated Fat	1 g
Cholesterol	4 mg
Sodium	136 mg
Carbohydrate	17 g
Fiber	1 g
Protein	4 g

EXCHANGES:
1 Starch
½ Fat

PREPARATION TIME: 25 minutes
RISING TIMES: 1hour; 30 minutes
RESTING TIME: 10 minutes
BAKING TIME: 35 minutes

TOTAL FAT: 2 g

DAILY VALUE FAT: 3%

SATURATED FAT: 0 g

DAILY VALUE SATURATED FAT: 0%

NUTRITION FACTS
PER SERVING:

Calories	147
Total Fat	2 g
Saturated Fat	0 g
Cholesterol	0 mg
Sodium	269 mg
Carbohydrate	28 g
Fiber	3 g
Protein	5 g

EXCHANGES:

2 Starch

PREPARATION TIME: 25 minutes

RISING TIMES: 45 minutes; 30 minutes

BAKING TIME: 35 minutes

Country Whole Wheat Bread

Italian bakers call this crusty whole wheat bread pan integrale. *The name refers to the unadulterated nature of whole wheat flour. Dip it in a little olive oil that is pooled on a plate and sprinkled with cracked pepper, coarse salt, or crushed herbs.*

1⅓ cups warm water (115° to 120°)
  1 package active dry yeast
  1 tablespoon olive oil
  2 teaspoons snipped fresh sage or
       ¼ teaspoon dried sage, crushed
1½ teaspoons salt
  1 teaspoon sugar
1½ cups whole wheat flour
  2 to 2½ cups bread or all-purpose flour

● In a large mixing bowl stir together warm water, yeast, oil, sage, salt, and sugar. Let mixture stand for 5 minutes.

● Using a wooden spoon, stir in the whole wheat flour, about ½ cup at a time. Add *1½ cups* of the bread or all-purpose flour, a little at a time, stirring until most of the flour has been absorbed and the dough begins to form a ball.

● On a lightly floured surface, knead in enough of the remaining bread or all-purpose flour to make a moderately stiff dough that is smooth and elastic (6 to 8 minutes total). Shape the dough into a ball. Place in a lightly greased bowl; turn once to grease the surface. Cover and let rise in a warm place until double (45 to 60 minutes).

● Punch dough down. Cover and let rest for 10 minutes. On a lightly greased baking sheet, shape dough into a 6×3-inch oval loaf. Sprinkle lightly with any remaining flour. Cover and let rise until almost double (30 to 45 minutes).

● Using a sharp knife, slash the top of the loaf several times, making each cut about ½ inch deep. Bake in a 425° oven. For a crisp crust, spray or brush with *cold water* every 3 minutes during the first 9 minutes of baking.

● After 9 minutes, reduce oven temperature to 375°; sprinkle the bread with any remaining all-purpose flour. Bake about 20 minutes more or until bread sounds hollow when tapped. (If necessary, cover loosely with foil the last 15 minutes of baking to prevent overbrowning.) Immediately remove bread from pan. Cool on a wire rack. Makes 1 loaf (12 servings).

Bread Machine Conversion Helps and Hints

Converting a bread recipe from the conventional method to one for your bread machine isn't difficult. Follow these tips:

● Reduce the amount of flour to 2 cups for a 1-pound machine or 3 cups for a 1½-pound machine.

● Reduce all ingredients by the same proportion, including the yeast (1 package equals about 2¼ teaspoons). If a range is given for flour, use the lower amount to figure the reduction proportion. For example, for a 1½-pound machine, a recipe calling for 4½ to 5 cups flour and 1 package yeast would be decreased by ⅓ cup to 3 cups flour and 1½ teaspoons yeast.

● If the bread uses 2 or more types of flour, add the flour amounts together and use that total as the basis for reducing the recipe. The total amount of flour used should be only 2 or 3 cups, depending on the size of your machine.

● Use bread flour instead of all-purpose flour or add 1 to 2 tablespoons gluten flour (available at health food stores) to the all-purpose flour.

● Make sure the liquids in the recipe are at room temperature before starting.

● Measure the ingredients as you would for any other recipe, but add them in the order specified by the bread machine manufacturer.

● Add dried fruits or nuts at the raisin bread cycle, if your machine has one. If not, add them according to the manufacturer's directions.

● Do not use light-colored fruits, such as apricots and golden raisins, because the preservatives added to them can inhibit the yeast performance. Choose another fruit or use the dough cycle and lightly knead in the fruit by hand before shaping the loaves. (Note: When using the machine to make the dough only, it may be necessary to knead in a little more flour after removing the dough from the bread machine and before shaping it. Knead in just enough additional flour to make the dough easy to handle. If necessary, let the dough rest 5 minutes before shaping it. The dough is extremely elastic and letting it rest makes it easier to shape.)

● For breads containing whole wheat or rye flour, use the whole wheat cycle, if your machine has one. For sweet or rich breads, use the light-color setting or sweet bread cycle, if your machine has one. Watch the bread carefully because with some machines, using the sweet bread cycle may result in a product that is slightly underdone or gummy in the center.

● The first time you try a new bread in your machine, watch and listen carefully. Check the dough after the first 3 to 5 minutes of kneading. If your machine works excessively hard during the mixing cycle, if the dough looks dry and crumbly, or if 2 or more balls of dough form, add 1 to 2 tablespoons of extra liquid. If the dough looks extremely soft and it won't form a ball, add more flour, 1 tablespoon at a time, until a dough ball does form. For your future reference, record how much additional liquid or flour you needed to add.

TOTAL FAT: 10 g
DAILY VALUE FAT: 15%
SATURATED FAT: 4 g
DAILY VALUE SATURATED FAT: 20%

NUTRITION FACTS
PER SERVING:

Calories	322
Total Fat	10 g
Saturated Fat	4 g
Cholesterol	79 mg
Sodium	562 mg
Carbohydrate	39 g
Fiber	1 g
Protein	19 g

EXCHANGES:

2 Starch
1½ Vegetable
1½ Lean Meat
1 Fat

PREPARATION TIME: 45 minutes
COOKING TIME: 45 minutes
COOLING TIME: 10 minutes

Pizza Rustica

Hot roll mix cuts down on the time to make this impressive and tasty stuffed pizza. Be sure to drain all liquid from the spinach so it doesn't add too much moisture to the crust or filling.

1 **16-ounce package hot roll mix**
1 **pound very lean ground beef**
1 **cup chopped onion**
1 **cup sliced fresh mushrooms**
2 **cloves garlic, minced**
¼ **teaspoon ground black pepper**
1 **8-ounce can pizza sauce**
½ **of a 7-ounce jar roasted red sweet peppers, drained and chopped**
1 **teaspoon dried Italian seasoning, crushed**
½ **cup shredded low-fat mozzarella cheese (2 ounces)**
¼ **cup freshly grated Parmesan cheese (1 ounce)**
1 **10-ounce package frozen chopped spinach, thawed and well drained**
2 **eggs, slightly beaten separately**
1 **tablespoon water**
2 **teaspoons sesame seed**

● Prepare hot roll mix according to package directions through the kneading step. Cover and let dough rest.

● Meanwhile, in a large skillet cook ground beef, onion, mushrooms, garlic, and black pepper until meat is brown and onion is tender. Drain well. Stir in pizza sauce, sweet peppers, and Italian seasoning. Cook and stir until heated through. Cover and keep warm.

● Spray the bottom of a 9-inch springform pan with nonstick coating. On a lightly floured surface, roll three-fourths of the dough into a 13-inch circle. Place dough in the springform pan (the dough will extend about 2½ inches up the sides). Press pleats in dough as necessary to fit. Sprinkle bottom of dough with *half* of each of the cheeses. Spoon meat mixture over cheese.

● Pat spinach dry with paper towels. Combine the spinach, *one* of the slightly beaten eggs, and the remaining cheeses. Spread spinach mixture over meat mixture. Roll remaining dough into a 9-inch circle; place over the spinach mixture. Fold excess bottom crust over top crust; crimp edge to seal. In a small bowl combine the remaining beaten egg and the water. Brush over the top of the dough. Sprinkle with sesame seed.

● Bake in a 350° oven for about 45 minutes or until golden brown. Cool 10 minutes on a wire rack. To serve, remove sides of springform pan; cut into wedges. Makes 10 main-dish servings.

TOTAL FAT: 12 g
DAILY VALUE FAT: 18%
SATURATED FAT: 4 g
DAILY VALUE SATURATED FAT: 20%

NUTRITION FACTS
PER SERVING:

Calories	334
Total Fat	12 g
Saturated Fat	4 g
Cholesterol	17 mg
Sodium	657 mg
Carbohydrate	42 g
Fiber	4 g
Protein	19 g

EXCHANGES:
2 Starch
2½ Vegetable
1 Medium-Fat Meat
1 Fat

PREPARATION TIME: 25 minutes
BAKING TIME: 20 minutes

Whole Wheat Pesto Pizza

We've included a recipe for a lower-fat pesto—it contains less oil than most already prepared types you'll find at the supermarket. Use purchased pesto when you're short on time, but use it sparingly. (Pictured on page 46.)

  1 **16-ounce loaf frozen whole wheat bread dough, thawed**
  1 **leek or green onion, thinly sliced**
  1 **small yellow summer squash or zucchini, halved and thinly sliced**
  ¼ **of a small yellow or green sweet pepper, cut into thin strips**
  ½ **cup pizza sauce**
1½ **cups shredded part-skim mozzarella cheese (6 ounces)**
  2 **Roma tomatoes, thinly sliced**
  ½ **cup sliced fresh mushrooms**
  ¼ **cup Pesto or purchased pesto**

● On a lightly floured surface, roll the bread dough into a 12-inch circle. Transfer dough to an 11-inch tart pan with a removable bottom. Press dough into bottom and up sides of pan. Prick generously with a fork. Bake in a 400° oven for 10 to 12 minutes or until light brown. Remove from oven.

● In a medium covered saucepan, cook the leek or green onion, squash or zucchini, and sweet pepper in a small amount of *boiling water* for 2 to 3 minutes or until tender; drain well.

● Spread pizza sauce over the crust. Sprinkle with *half* of the cheese. Arrange leek mixture, tomatoes, and mushrooms over cheese. Top with remaining cheese.

● Bake for 10 to 15 minutes more or until cheese melts and pizza is heated through. Crumble Pesto over top of hot pizza. Makes 6 main-dish servings.

Pesto: In a blender container or food processor bowl, combine 1 cup firmly packed *fresh basil leaves;* ½ cup torn *fresh spinach leaves;* ¼ cup grated *Parmesan* or *Romano cheese;* ¼ cup *pine nuts* or *almonds;* 2 cloves *garlic,* quartered; and, if desired, ¼ teaspoon *salt.* Cover and blend or process with several on-off turns until a paste forms, stopping the machine several times and scraping sides. With machine running slowly, gradually add 2 tablespoons *olive oil* or *cooking oil* and 2 tablespoons *water;* blend or process until mixture is the consistency of soft butter. Transfer mixture to a storage container. Cover and refrigerate for up to 2 days or freeze for up to 1 month. Makes ½ cup.

Pizza Margherita

As the story goes, this pizza was created in 1889 in honor of a late-19th-century Italian queen.
It represents Italy's flag with the colors green, red, and white.

1 recipe Pizza Crust or one 16-ounce
    Italian bread shell (Boboli)
1 cup shredded reduced-fat mozzarella
    cheese (4 ounces)
2 tablespoons snipped fresh basil
    or 1 teaspoon dried basil, crushed
4 fresh Roma tomatoes or 2 medium
    tomatoes, cut into thin wedges
    Olive oil nonstick spray coating or
    1 teaspoon olive oil

● Prebake Pizza Crust as directed at right.
Remove from oven. Sprinkle cheese over crust.
Sprinkle basil over all. Arrange the tomato
wedges in a circular pattern around the edge of
the crust and then in the center. Spray tomatoes
with nonstick coating or drizzle with olive
oil. Bake in a 425° oven for 10 to 15 minutes
or until hot. Serve pizza immediately. Makes
6 main-dish servings.

Pizza Crust

1½ to 2 cups bread flour or all-purpose
    flour
½ package (about 1¼ teaspoons) active dry
    yeast
¼ teaspoon garlic salt
½ cup warm water (120° to 130°)
1 tablespoon olive oil or cooking oil
    Cornmeal (optional)

● In a medium mixing bowl combine ¾ *cup* of
the flour, the yeast, and garlic salt. Add water
and oil. Beat with an electric mixer on low speed
for 30 seconds, scraping the bowl. Beat on high
speed for 3 minutes. Using a wooden spoon, stir
in as much of the remaining flour as you can.
On a lightly floured surface, knead in enough
of the remaining flour to make a moderately
stiff dough that is smooth and elastic (6 to
8 minutes). Cover and let rest 10 minutes.

● Grease one 12-inch pizza pan or large baking
sheet. If desired, sprinkle with cornmeal. Roll
and stretch the dough into a 13-inch circle.
Transfer to prepared pan. Build up edges slightly.
Do not let rise. Prebake crust in a 425° oven
about 12 minutes or until lightly browned.

TOTAL FAT: 8 g
DAILY VALUE FAT: 12%
SATURATED FAT: 2 g
DAILY VALUE SATURATED FAT: 10%

NUTRITION FACTS
PER SERVING:

Calories	269
Total Fat	8 g
Saturated Fat	2 g
Cholesterol	14 mg
Sodium	581 mg
Carbohydrate	38 g
Fiber	2 g
Protein	14 g

EXCHANGES:
2 Starch
1 Vegetable
1 Medium-Fat Meat
½ Fat

PREPARATION TIME: 12 minutes
BAKING TIME: 12 minutes

Peasant Pizza with
Goat Cheese

Using a small amount of goat cheese on this pizza adds a tangy flavor. Look for it in the specialty cheese section of the supermarket labeled "chèvre" (pronounced SHEV), which means goat in French.

1 16-ounce Italian bread shell (Boboli)
2 ounces fat-free cream cheese (block style) (about 2 ounces)
2 ounces semisoft goat cheese or feta cheese, crumbled (about ¼ cup)
1 teaspoon dried basil, crushed, or 2 tablespoons snipped fresh basil
1 clove garlic, minced
⅛ teaspoon ground black pepper
3 plum tomatoes, thinly sliced
1 small yellow, orange, or green sweet pepper, cut into thin bite-size strips

● Place the Italian bread shell on a baking sheet.

● In a small mixing bowl stir together the cream cheese, goat cheese or feta cheese, dried basil (if using), garlic, and black pepper. Spread over the bread shell. Place the tomato slices and sweet pepper strips over the cheese mixture.

● Bake pizza in a 400° oven about 12 minutes or until heated through. Sprinkle with the fresh basil (if using). To serve, cut into wedges. Makes 6 main-dish servings.

TOTAL FAT: 12 g
DAILY VALUE FAT: 18%
SATURATED FAT: 4 g
DAILY VALUE SATURATED FAT: 20%

**NUTRITION FACTS
PER SERVING:**

Calories	327
Total Fat	12 g
Saturated Fat	4 g
Cholesterol	37 mg
Sodium	373 mg
Carbohydrate	36 g
Fiber	3 g
Protein	19 g

EXCHANGES:
2 Starch
1 Vegetable
1½ Lean Meat
1 Fat

**PREPARATION TIME: 20 minutes
BAKING TIME: 20 minutes**

"Sausage" Pizza

Instead of using real sausage, which is generally high in fat, saturated fat, and calories, this pizza gets a makeover by using lean beef and adding the spices found in sausage.

1 recipe Garlic and Herb Pizza Dough or
  two 10-inch packaged prebaked (thin)
  pizza crusts
12 ounces extra-lean ground beef or ground
  chicken
1 teaspoon paprika
½ to 1 teaspoon crushed red pepper
½ teaspoon dried thyme, crushed
½ teaspoon fennel seed, crushed
¼ teaspoon salt
⅛ teaspoon ground black pepper
1 15-ounce or two 8-ounce can(s)
  low-sodium tomato sauce
2 tablespoons tomato paste
1 cup shredded part-skim mozzarella
  cheese (4 ounces)
¼ cup grated Parmesan or Romano cheese

● Prepare the Garlic and Herb Dough (if using). Grease two 11- or 12-inch pizza pans or large baking sheets. On a lightly floured surface, roll each half of dough into a circle 1 inch larger than the pizza pans, or roll into a 12-inch circle if using baking sheets. Transfer to prepared pans. Build up edges slightly. Flute edges, if desired. Prick the dough generously with a fork.

● Bake crust in a 425° oven for 10 to 12 minutes or until lightly browned. Remove from oven. (Or, place the partially baked purchased crusts in pizza pans or on baking sheets.)

● Meanwhile, in a large skillet cook the beef or chicken until no longer pink. Drain well. Stir in paprika, red pepper, thyme, fennel seed, salt, and black pepper. Set aside. Stir together tomato sauce and tomato paste. Spread sauce over hot crust. Sprinkle with meat mixture and cheeses. Bake for 10 to 12 minutes or until bubbly and cheese melts. Makes 8 servings.

Garlic and Herb Pizza Dough: In a large bowl combine 1¼ cups *all-purpose flour;* 2 cloves minced *garlic;* 1 package *active dry yeast;* 2 teaspoons *dried basil, oregano,* or *Italian seasoning,* crushed; and ½ teaspoon *salt.* Add 1 cup *warm water* (120° to 130°) and 2 tablespoons *olive* or *cooking oil.* Beat with an electric mixer on low speed 30 seconds, scraping bowl constantly. Beat on high speed 3 minutes. Using a spoon, stir in as much of 1¼ to 1¾ cups of *all-purpose flour* as you can. On a lightly floured surface, knead in enough of any remaining flour to make a moderately stiff dough that is smooth and elastic (6 to 8 minutes). Divide dough in half. Cover; let rest 10 minutes.

Calzones

Calzones (kal-ZOH-nays) are like savory turnovers. Using packaged refrigerated pizza dough makes these calzones quick to prepare.

    8 ounces very lean ground beef or ground
          turkey
    ½ cup sliced fresh mushrooms
    ¼ cup chopped green pepper
    ½ cup shredded reduced-fat mozzarella
          cheese (2 ounces)
    ⅓ cup pizza sauce
    1 10-ounce package refrigerated pizza
          dough
    1 tablespoon milk
       Grated Parmesan cheese (optional)
       Warmed pizza sauce (optional)

● In a medium skillet cook ground beef or turkey, mushrooms, and green pepper until meat is no longer pink. Drain well. Stir in the cheese and the ⅓ cup pizza sauce.

● For calzones, unroll pizza dough. Roll or stretch dough into a 15×10-inch rectangle. Cut dough into six 5-inch squares. Divide the meat mixture among the squares. Brush edges with *water.* Lift a corner and stretch dough over to opposite corner. Seal the edges by pressing with the tines of a fork.

● Place on a greased baking sheet. Prick tops with a fork to allow steam to escape. Brush with the milk. If desired, sprinkle with Parmesan cheese. Bake in a 425° oven for 8 to 10 minutes or until golden brown. Let stand for 5 minutes before serving. If desired, serve with warmed pizza sauce. Makes 6 main-dish servings.

A Better Beef

Cook with the leanest ground beef available to keep your low-fat goals in check. Look for 90-percent lean (10-percent fat). Some supermarkets offer 95-percent lean ground beef. This type of ground beef has some of the fat replaced with water and plant derivatives. Use lean ground beef for meatballs and in sauces, casseroles, and any other recipe that calls for ground beef.

TOTAL FAT: 7 g
DAILY VALUE FAT: 10%
SATURATED FAT: 3 g
DAILY VALUE SATURATED FAT: 15%

**NUTRITION FACTS
PER SERVING:**

Calories	224
Total Fat	7 g
Saturated Fat	3 g
Cholesterol	29 mg
Sodium	355 mg
Carbohydrate	23 g
Fiber	0 g
Protein	14 g

EXCHANGES:
1½ Starch
½ Vegetable
1½ Lean Meat
½ Fat

PREPARATION TIME: 20 minutes
BAKING TIME: 9 minutes
STANDING TIME: 5 minutes

TOTAL FAT: 9 g
DAILY VALUE FAT: 13%
SATURATED FAT: 5 g
DAILY VALUE SATURATED FAT: 25%

NUTRITION FACTS
PER SERVING:

Calories	325
Total Fat	9 g
Saturated Fat	5 g
Cholesterol	92 mg
Sodium	292 mg
Carbohydrate	41 g
Fiber	2 g
Protein	20 g

EXCHANGES:
2½ Starch
1 Vegetable
1½ Medium-Fat Meat

PREPARATION TIME: 20 minutes
CHILLING TIME: 2 hours
BAKING TIME: 20 minutes

Tomato Polenta Pizza

Semolina is a type of wheat flour used in making pasta. Look for it in the baking section of your supermarket.

3   cups skim milk
1½ cups fine semolina (pasta flour)
2   beaten eggs
½   cup finely shredded Asiago or Parmesan
       cheese (2 ounces)
⅛   teaspoon salt
⅛   teaspoon pepper
       Nonstick spray coating
4   plum tomatoes, very thinly sliced
4   ounces mozzarella cheese, thinly sliced
1   tablespoon seasoned fine dry bread
       crumbs

● For crust, in a large saucepan bring milk just to boiling over medium heat. Sprinkle the semolina over the milk, stirring constantly. Cook and stir for 2 minutes. Remove from heat. Cool 5 minutes. Stir in the eggs, Asiago or Parmesan cheese, salt, and pepper.

● Spray a 12-inch pizza pan with nonstick coating. Spread the semolina mixture into the pan. Cover and chill for 2 to 24 hours. Arrange tomato slices over the top. Cover tomatoes with sliced cheese. Sprinkle with bread crumbs.

● Bake pizza in a 400° oven for 20 minutes or until cheese is melted and beginning to brown. Serve immediately. Makes 6 main-dish servings.

Spray for Success

Nonstick spray coating not only bypasses the mess of greasing pans but also saves on fat. A 1¼-second spray replaces a tablespoon of margarine or butter and contains only 0.8 grams of fat (a tablespoon of margarine contains 10 grams of fat). Here are a few tips for using nonstick spray coating:

● Hold pans over your sink or garbage when spraying so you don't make your floor or counter slippery.
● Spray only onto cold baking pans or skillets. Cooking spray can burn or smoke if sprayed onto hot surfaces.
● Keep pasta water from bubbling over by spraying the pan first.

TOTAL FAT: 5 g
DAILY VALUE FAT: 7%
SATURATED FAT: 5 g
DAILY VALUE SATURATED FAT: 25%

NUTRITION FACTS
PER SERVING:

Calories	410
Total Fat	13 g
Saturated Fat	5 g
Cholesterol	59 mg
Sodium	724 mg
Carbohydrate	45 g
Fiber	1 g
Protein	26 g

EXCHANGES:
2½ Starch
2 Vegetable
2½ Medium-Fat Meat

PREPARATION TIME: 20 minutes
COOKING TIME: 15 minutes

Spicy Italian "Sausage"
Sandwich

Instead of using fatty sausage for this popular sandwich, we just used the spices that make sausage taste like sausage—fennel seed, paprika, garlic, and red peppers.

1   **16-ounce loaf unsliced Italian or French bread (about 16×4 inches) or 6 individual French rolls**
1   **pound extra-lean ground pork or beef**
1   **cup sliced fresh mushrooms**
¾   **cup chopped onion**
½   **cup chopped green sweet pepper**
1   **garlic clove, minced**
1   **or 2 dried red chili peppers, crushed**
1   **teaspoon paprika**
½   **teaspoon dried thyme, crushed**
½   **teaspoon fennel seed, crushed**
¼   **teaspoon salt**
⅛   **teaspoon ground black pepper**
1   **8-ounce can low-sodium tomato sauce***
2   **tablespoons grated Parmesan cheese**
¾   **cup shredded reduced-fat mozzarella cheese (3 ounces)**

● Split bread loaf in half horizontally. Hollow out bottom half of the loaf, leaving about 1-inch shell. (If using individual rolls, hollow them out slightly.) Set aside. (Reserve the bread pieces from inside of the loaf for another use, such as bread crumbs.)

● In a large skillet cook pork or beef, mushrooms, onion, sweet pepper, and garlic until no pink remains in pork. Drain well. Stir in the red chili peppers, paprika, thyme, fennel seed, salt, and black pepper. Stir in the tomato sauce. Heat to boiling; reduce heat. Cover and simmer for 10 minutes. Stir in Parmesan cheese.

● Spoon meat mixture into the bottom half of the bread loaf or rolls. Sprinkle mozzarella cheese over the meat mixture; cover with loaf or roll top(s). Place sandwich in a shallow baking pan or on a baking sheet. Cover tightly with foil and bake in a 375° oven for 15 to 20 minutes or until cheese melts and sandwich is hot. (For smaller sandwiches, wrap each in foil and place on a baking sheet or in a shallow baking pan. Bake in a 300° oven for 10 minutes to warm.)

● To serve the large sandwich, use a serrated knife to slice the loaf crosswise into 6 portions. Makes 6 main-dish servings.

Note: By using this low-sodium product instead of regular tomato sauce, you reduce the sodium in an individual serving by about 225 milligrams.

Pepper and Cheese Sandwich

You can use all green sweet peppers in this sandwich if you like. The various types of peppers, however, will make it more colorful.

2   **medium onions, thinly sliced and separated into rings**
1   **medium green sweet pepper, cut into thin strips**
1   **medium red sweet pepper, cut into thin strips**
1   **medium yellow sweet pepper, cut into thin strips**
2   **cloves garlic, minced**
1   **teaspoon dried basil, crushed, or 1 tablespoon snipped fresh basil**
2   **teaspoons olive oil**
6   **individual French bread loaves**
8   **ounces reduced-fat mozzarella or provolone cheese, sliced**

● In a large covered skillet cook onions, sweet pepper strips, garlic, and dried basil (if using) in hot oil over medium heat for 8 to 10 minutes or until vegetables are tender, stirring occasionally.

● Meanwhile, split loaves in half horizontally, slicing to, but not through, the other side. Hollow out loaves, leaving about ½-inch shell. (Reserve bread for another use.) Place opened loaves on a broiler pan. Arrange *half* the cheese in the bottom of loaves. Divide vegetables mixture over cheese. Top with remaining cheese. Broil 3 to 4 inches from heat for 1 to 2 minutes or until cheese is melted. Remove from oven. Sprinkle with fresh basil (if using). Fold bread tops over cheese. Makes 6 main-dish servings.

Say Cheese

Cheesy lasagna, pizzas, and calzones are just a few of the Italian dishes Americans love. To hold down the fat content in these wonderful dishes, look for lower-fat and nonfat natural and process cheeses. Here are some to consider:

● Reduced-fat natural cheese is a natural cheese, such as cheddar, Swiss, and Monterey jack, with fewer grams of fat than regular natural cheese. Lower-fat mozzarella is called "part-skim mozzarella cheese."
● Lower-fat flavored process cheese product is a lower-fat process cheese that is available in American, cheddar, or Swiss flavors.
● Nonfat process cheese product is a process cheese without any fat.

TOTAL FAT: 10 g
DAILY VALUE FAT: 15%
SATURATED FAT: 5 g
DAILY VALUE SATURATED FAT: 25%

NUTRITION FACTS
PER SERVING:

Calories	351
Total Fat	10 g
Saturated Fat	5 g
Cholesterol	20 mg
Sodium	648 mg
Carbohydrate	47 g
Fiber	4 g
Protein	18 g

EXCHANGES:
2½ Starch
1½ Vegetable
1½ Lean Meat
1 Fat

PREPARATION TIME: 30 minutes
COOKING TIME: 1 to 2 minutes

Grilled Vegetables on Focaccia

When grilled, vegetables take on a pleasant smoky flavor. Lay the vegetables perpendicular to the wires on the grill rack so the vegetables don't fall into the coals.

3 tablespoons balsamic vinegar or wine
    vinegar
2 tablespoons water
1 tablespoon olive oil
1 teaspoon dried oregano, crushed
2 large red and/or yellow sweet peppers
2 medium zucchini, halved crosswise and
    sliced thinly lengthwise
1 medium eggplant, cut crosswise into
    ½-inch slices
2 ounces soft goat cheese (chèvre)
2 ounces fat-free cream cheese
1 recipe Easy Herb Focaccia (see recipe,
    page 54) or purchased focaccia (about
    a 12-inch round)

● In a small bowl combine vinegar, water, oil, and oregano. Set aside. Cut sweet peppers in quarters. Remove stems, membranes, and seeds. Arrange all vegetables on grill rack directly over medium-hot coals; brush with vinegar mixture. Grill, uncovered, until slightly charred, turning occasionally (allow 8 to 10 minutes for peppers and eggplant, and 5 to 6 minutes for zucchini). Cut peppers into strips.

● In a small bowl combine the goat cheese and cream cheese. Set aside.

● Split each 9-inch Easy Herb Focaccia into 2 layers horizontally. (Or, if using purchased focaccia, cut in half crosswise. Split halves into 2 layers horizontally to form 4 pieces total.) Spread goat cheese mixture over bottom layers of focaccia; top with some of the sweet peppers, zucchini, and eggplant; place top halves of focaccia over vegetables. To serve, cut into wedges. Makes 8 main-dish servings.

TOTAL FAT: 10 g
DAILY VALUE FAT: 15%
SATURATED FAT: 2 g
DAILY VALUE SATURATED FAT: 5%

NUTRITION FACTS
PER SERVING:

Calories	324
Total Fat	10 g
Saturated Fat	2 g
Cholesterol	31 mg
Sodium	470 mg
Carbohydrate	51 g
Fiber	2 g
Protein	10 g

EXCHANGES:
3 Starch
1 Vegetable
½ Lean Meat
1 Fat

PREPARATION TIME: 20 minutes
COOKING TIME: 8 minutes

Chicken with Pumpkin and Zucchini, recipe on page 76

Pasta alla Carbonara with Asparagus,
recipe on page 84

Main Dishes

You'll find so many tantalizing recipes in this chapter you won't know where to begin. May we suggest the hearty Garlic-Sage-Marinated Beef Pot Roast (page 87)—perfect for warming any winter chills? If you have a passion for pasta, try the Baked Cavatelli (page 92) or the ever-favorite Spaghetti with Italian Meatballs (page 89). Classics, such as Osso Buco (page 94), Bolognese Meat Sauce with Pasta (page 90), and Veal Scaloppine with Marsala (page 96), also shouldn't be missed. But many authentic renditions will make new recipe favorites, such as Chicken with Artichokes (page 82) and Italian Pork Roast (page 102).

TOTAL FAT: 10 g
DAILY VALUE FAT: 15%
SATURATED FAT: 3 g
DAILY VALUE SATURATED FAT: 15%

NUTRITION FACTS
PER SERVING:

Calories	266
Total Fat	10 g
Saturated Fat	3 g
Cholesterol	66 mg
Sodium	157 mg
Carbohydrate	17 g
Fiber	2 g
Protein	22 g

EXCHANGES:
1 Starch
½ Vegetable
3 Lean Meat

PREPARATION TIME: 20 minutes
COOKING TIME: 50 minutes

Chicken with Pumpkin
And Zucchini

This one-pot meal makes cleanup a snap. Serve this dish with a crisp green salad, crusty bread, and fresh fruit for dessert. (Pictured on page 74.)

1   2½- to 3-pound meaty chicken pieces,
      cut up and skinned
      Nonstick spray coating
¼   cup finely chopped onion
2   cloves garlic, minced
2   medium potatoes, peeled and cut in
      1-inch cubes
2   cups peeled, 1-inch cubes pumpkin or
      winter squash
⅔   cup dry white wine or reduced-sodium
      chicken broth
1   teaspoon dried rosemary, crushed
¼   teaspoon salt
¼   teaspoon pepper
2   medium zucchini, sliced ¼ inch thick
      Lemon wedges (optional)

● Rinse chicken; pat dry with paper towels. Spray an unheated 12-inch skillet with nonstick coating. Preheat skillet over medium heat. Add the chicken and cook for 10 to 15 minutes or until lightly brown, turning to brown evenly and adding onion and garlic during the last 5 minutes of cooking. Add the potatoes and pumpkin or winter squash.

● Combine wine or broth, rosemary, salt, and pepper; pour over chicken and vegetables. Bring mixture to boiling; reduce heat. Cover and simmer for 25 minutes. Add zucchini. Cover and cook about 5 minutes more or until chicken and vegetables are tender and chicken is no longer pink. Using a slotted spoon, transfer chicken and vegetables to a serving platter. Pass pan juices. If desired, serve with lemon wedges. Makes 6 servings.

Which Squash Is Which?

Generally, squash is classified as summer or winter. Today, both types are available throughout the year. When looking for winter squash, seek out acorn, banana, buttercup, butternut, delicata, hubbard, or turban. Summer squash includes pattypan, sunburst, yellow, and zucchini. Pumpkin may be used in recipes that call for winter squash.

Roasted Peppers
And Chicken Skillet

Roasted peppers add color and sweetness to this dish, but they're also an outstanding source of vitamin A. Make them up ahead (see tip*) to save time when preparing this dish.

2 large yellow, red, and/or green
　　sweet peppers
2 pounds meaty chicken pieces (breasts,
　　thighs, and drumsticks), skinned
1 tablespoon olive oil
1 teaspoon dried oregano, crushed
¼ teaspoon salt
　　Dash crushed red pepper
1 cup chopped onion
¾ cup thinly sliced celery
¾ cup dry white wine or reduced-sodium
　　chicken broth
1 14½-ounce can tomatoes, cut up
2 cups hot cooked rice

● To roast the sweet peppers, cut them into quarters. Remove stems, membranes, and seeds. Place pepper pieces, cut side down, on a baking sheet lined with foil. Bake in a 425° oven 20 to 25 minutes or until skins are bubbly and very dark. Wrap pepper pieces tightly in foil and let stand for 10 to 15 minutes or until cool enough to handle. Using a paring knife, pull the skin off gently. Cut into ½-inch-wide strips. Set aside.

● Rinse chicken; pat dry with paper towels. In a large nonstick skillet cook chicken in hot oil over medium heat for 10 to 15 minutes or until lightly browned, turning to brown evenly. Drain well. Sprinkle chicken with oregano, salt, and crushed red pepper. Stir in the onion, celery, and wine or broth. Bring to boiling.

● Cook, uncovered, over high heat for 10 to 15 minutes or until most of the liquid has evaporated, turning chicken once. Carefully stir in the *undrained* tomatoes. Meanwhile, begin preparing rice.

● Cover skillet and simmer chicken for 15 minutes. Stir in the roasted pepper strips. Cook, uncovered, about 5 minutes more or until chicken is tender and no longer pink and sauce is of desired consistency. Serve over hot rice. Makes 4 servings.

*Test Kitchen's Make-Ahead Tip: Prepare roasted sweet peppers as directed and place individual pepper pieces between sheets of waxed paper. Place in a sealable plastic freezer bag; freeze for up to 3 months. To use, thaw at room temperature about 30 minutes. (Or, place the peppers and a small amount of olive oil in an airtight container. Refrigerate for up to 1 week.)

TOTAL FAT: 10 g
DAILY VALUE FAT: 15%
SATURATED FAT: 2 g
DAILY VALUE SATURATED FAT: 10%

NUTRITION FACTS
PER SERVING:

Calories	441
Total Fat	10 g
Saturated Fat	2 g
Cholesterol	93 mg
Sodium	411 mg
Carbohydrate	43 g
Fiber	5 g
Protein	36 g

EXCHANGES:
2 Starch
3½ Lean Meat
2½ Vegetable

PREPARATION TIME: 1 hour
COOKING TIME: 35 minutes

Chicken with Golden Raisins And Pine Nuts

Italians frequently use pine nuts, also called pignoli, in pasta sauces, pesto, rice dishes and cookies. Refrigerate pine nuts in an airtight container for up to two months or freeze them for up to six months to prevent them from turning rancid quickly at room temperature.

1½ pounds meaty chicken pieces (breasts, thighs, and drumsticks), skinned
1 medium onion, cut into thin slivers
2 cloves garlic, minced
1 tablespoon olive oil
½ cup white wine vinegar
¼ teaspoon salt
⅛ teaspoon pepper
1 cup reduced-sodium chicken broth
½ cup golden raisins
2 teaspoons snipped fresh thyme or
  ½ teaspoon dried thyme, crushed
1 teaspoon snipped fresh rosemary or
  ¼ teaspoon dried rosemary, crushed
1 tablespoon cold water
1½ teaspoons cornstarch
2 tablespoons toasted pine nuts

● Rinse chicken; pat dry with paper towels. In a large nonstick skillet cook onion and garlic in hot oil over medium heat for 1 minute. Add chicken pieces to skillet and cook for 10 to 15 minutes or until lightly browned, turning to brown evenly. Drain well.

● Add the vinegar, salt, and pepper to skillet. Bring to boiling. Cook, uncovered, over high heat about 5 minutes or until vinegar is nearly evaporated, turning chicken once. Carefully add broth, raisins, thyme, and rosemary to the skillet. Bring to boiling; reduce heat. Cover and simmer for 30 to 35 minutes or until chicken is tender and no longer pink. To serve, transfer chicken to a serving platter. Combine cold water and cornstarch. Add to skillet. Cook and stir until thickened and bubbly; cook and stir 2 minutes more. Spoon some of the sauce over chicken; pass remainder. Sprinkle chicken with pine nuts. Makes 4 servings.

TOTAL FAT: 10 g
DAILY VALUE FAT: 15%
SATURATED FAT: 2 g
DAILY VALUE SATURATED FAT: 10%

NUTRITION FACTS PER SERVING:

Calories	269
Total Fat	10 g
Saturated Fat	2 g
Cholesterol	71 mg
Sodium	334 mg
Carbohydrate	22 g
Fiber	1 g
Protein	24 g

EXCHANGES:
1½ Fruit
3 Lean Meat

PREPARATION TIME: 8 minutes
COOKING TIME: 55 minutes

TOTAL FAT: 14 g

DAILY VALUE FAT: 22%

SATURATED FAT: 7 g

DAILY VALUE SATURATED FAT: 35%

NUTRITION FACTS
PER SERVING:

Calories	318
Total Fat	14 g
Saturated Fat	7 g
Cholesterol	76 mg
Sodium	291 mg
Carbohydrate	24 g
Fiber	1 g
Protein	23 g

EXCHANGES:

1½ Starch

1 Vegetable

2½ Lean Meat

1 Fat

PREPARATION TIME: 40 minutes

COOKING TIME: 30 minutes

Chicken Manicotti
With Red Pepper Cream Sauce

Reduced-fat cream cheese and skim milk combine to make a creamy sauce with a fraction of the fat of traditional cream sauces.

12 **manicotti or 18 conchiglioni (jumbo shells)**

1 **8-ounce package reduced-fat cream cheese (Neufchâtel), cut up**

¾ **cup skim milk**

½ **of a 7-ounce jar roasted red sweet peppers (about ½ cup), drained and chopped, or one 4-ounce jar diced pimiento, drained**

3 **tablespoons grated Parmesan cheese**

1 **9-ounce package (2 cups) frozen diced cooked chicken, thawed**

1 **10-ounce package frozen chopped broccoli, thawed and drained**

2 **tablespoons thinly sliced green onion**

¼ **teaspoon ground black pepper**

● Cook pasta according to package directions. Rinse with cold water; drain well.

● Meanwhile, for sauce, in a heavy small saucepan stir cream cheese and ¼ cup of the milk over medium-low heat until smooth. Stir in remaining milk. Stir in sweet peppers or pimiento and Parmesan cheese; heat through.

● For filling, in a large bowl stir together ¾ cup of the sauce (set remaining sauce aside), the chicken, broccoli, onion, and black pepper. Using a small spoon, stuff each manicotti with about ¼ cup of the filling or each conchiglioni with 2 to 3 tablespoons filling. Place in a 3-quart rectangular baking dish. Bake, covered, in a 350° oven for 30 minutes or until heated through.

● To serve, cook and stir remaining sauce over low heat until heated through. Place 2 manicotti or 3 shells on each serving plate. Spoon sauce over shells. Makes 6 servings.

Cooked Chicken Choices

When a recipe calls for cooked chicken, you can purchase a package of frozen diced cooked chicken (as called for in the recipe above). Or, purchase a deli-roasted chicken. A cooked chicken will yield 1½ to 2 cups boneless chopped meat. If you have more time, you can poach chicken breasts. For 2 cups cubed cooked chicken, in a large skillet place 12 ounces skinless, boneless chicken breasts and 1½ cups water. Bring to boiling; reduce heat. Cover and simmer for 12 to 14 minutes or until chicken is tender and no longer pink. Drain well. Cut up the chicken.

Rosemary-Lemon
Roast Chicken

All you need is four ingredients for this simply delicious roasted chicken. Roast some whole cloves of garlic in the oven with the chicken (wrap them in foil with a little olive oil and bake about 30 minutes) and whip them into mashed potatoes for a mouthwatering side dish—no need for gravy or butter.

1 **3-pound broiler-fryer chicken**
2 **cloves garlic, minced**
2 **tablespoons snipped fresh rosemary or**
    2 teaspoons dried rosemary, crushed
1 **medium lemon**
    Salt

● Rinse chicken; pat dry with paper towels. Combine garlic and rosemary. Rub chicken inside and out with garlic mixture. Halve and juice lemon. Sprinkle *2 tablespoons* lemon juice over prepared chicken. Sprinkle chicken with salt. Place the squeezed lemon halves in body cavity.

● Skewer neck skin to back. Tie legs to tail; twist wing tips under back. Place chicken, breast side up, on rack in shallow roasting pan. Insert meat thermometer in center of inside thigh muscle, making sure bulb does not touch bone. Bake, uncovered, in a 375° oven for 1¼ to 1½ hours or until meat thermometer registers 185° and drumsticks move easily in their sockets, brushing occasionally with drippings. Makes 6 servings.

Skip the Skin

To cut down on fat, remove skin from poultry before you serve it. It's OK to leave the skin on during cooking because it adds flavor and keeps moistness in, yet the meat won't absorb much of the fat. For comparison, take a look at the difference between a 3.5-ounce serving of roasted chicken served with skin and without.

	Fat (grams)	Calories
Light meat with skin	11	222
Light meat without skin	5	173

TOTAL FAT: 8 g
DAILY VALUE FAT: 12%
SATURATED FAT: 2 g
DAILY VALUE SATURATED FAT: 10%

NUTRITION FACTS
PER SERVING:

Calories	209
Total Fat	8 g
Saturated Fat	2 g
Cholesterol	96 mg
Sodium	93 mg
Carbohydrate	1 g
Fiber	0 g
Protein	31 g

EXCHANGES:
4 Lean Meat

PREPARATION TIME: 15 minutes
COOKING TIME: 1¼ hours

TOTAL FAT: 13 g
DAILY VALUE FAT: 19%
SATURATED FAT: 3 g
DAILY VALUE SATURATED FAT: 15%

**NUTRITION FACTS
PER SERVING:**

Calories	286
Total Fat	13 g
Saturated Fat	3 g
Cholesterol	70 mg
Sodium	427 mg
Carbohydrate	18 g
Fiber	5 g
Protein	26 g

EXCHANGES:
3 Vegetable
3 Lean Meat
1 Fat

**PREPARATION TIME: 20 minutes
COOKING TIME: 45 minutes**

Chicken with Artichokes

Italians have cultivated and enjoyed artichokes since early Roman times. Using frozen artichokes in this dish is convenient because all inedible parts are already removed.

1½ pounds meaty chicken pieces (breasts, thighs, and drumsticks), skinned
¼ teaspoon salt
⅛ teaspoon pepper
½ cup dried tomatoes (not oil-pack)
1 large leek, thinly sliced, or ⅓ cup chopped onion
2 cups sliced fresh mushrooms
2 cloves garlic, minced
½ teaspoon dried rosemary, crushed, or 2 teaspoons snipped fresh rosemary
2 tablespoons olive oil
¾ cup chicken broth
1 teaspoon finely shredded lemon peel
3 tablespoons lemon juice
1 8- or 9-ounce package frozen artichoke hearts

● Rinse chicken; pat dry with paper towels. Sprinkle chicken pieces with salt and pepper. Using scissors, cut dried tomatoes into thin strips. Set aside.

● In a large skillet cook leek or onion, mushrooms, garlic, and dried rosemary (if using), in hot oil until leek is tender. Remove with slotted spoon; set aside. Add chicken pieces to the skillet and cook over medium heat for 10 minutes, turning to brown evenly. Add tomatoes, leek mixture, broth, lemon peel, and lemon juice to the skillet. Bring to boiling; reduce heat. Cover and simmer for 20 minutes.

● Meanwhile, thaw artichoke hearts under cold water just enough to separate them. Drain. Halve any large artichokes. Add to skillet along with fresh rosemary (if using). Return to boiling; reduce heat. Cover and simmer for 10 to 15 minutes or until chicken is tender and no longer pink. To serve, transfer chicken and vegetables to a serving platter. Makes 4 servings.

TOTAL FAT: 10 g
DAILY VALUE FAT: 15%
SATURATED FAT: 3 g
DAILY VALUE SATURATED FAT: 15%

NUTRITION FACTS
PER SERVING:

Calories	410
Total Fat	10 g
Saturated Fat	3 g
Cholesterol	20 mg
Sodium	512 mg
Carbohydrate	56 g
Fiber	4 g
Protein	23 g

EXCHANGES:
3 Starch
1 Vegetable
2 Lean Meat
½ Milk
1 Fat

PREPARATION TIME: 22 minutes
COOKING TIME: 6 minutes

Pasta alla Carbonara
With Asparagus

Traditionally, a raw egg is used in this sauce. By substituting a pasteurized egg product, you can be sure your dish will be safe for you and your family. If you can't find pecorino cheese, which is made from sheep's milk (see glossary on page 11), Parmesan cheese is a suitable substitute. (Pictured on pages 74 and 75.)

2 cups 1-inch pieces asparagus or one 10-ounce package of frozen cut asparagus
3 slices turkey bacon or bacon, sliced crosswise into thin strips
1 clove garlic, minced
1 cup evaporated skim milk
¼ cup refrigerated or frozen egg product, thawed
8 ounces packaged dried fusilli, spaghetti, or fettuccine
2 teaspoons margarine
½ cup freshly grated pecorino or Parmesan cheese
¼ cup snipped fresh parsley
Freshly ground black pepper

● In a small saucepan cook fresh asparagus in a small amount of boiling *water* for 4 to 6 minutes or until crisp tender. (Or, cook the frozen asparagus according to package directions.) Drain and set aside.

● In a small nonstick skillet cook bacon and garlic until bacon is crisp. Drain on paper towels. Set aside. In a medium bowl stir together the milk and egg product. Set aside.

● Cook pasta according to package directions, *except* omit the cooking oil and salt. Drain well. Return to hot kettle. Immediately pour the egg mixture over the pasta. Add the margarine. Heat and stir mixture over medium-low heat for 5 to 6 minutes or until mixture thickens and pasta is well coated. Add the asparagus, cooked bacon mixture, cheese, and parsley; toss until combined. To serve, transfer pasta to a large serving dish. Sprinkle with black pepper. Makes 4 servings.

Lighter Lasagna

Compared to regular lasagna, this version saves you half the fat and 125 calories per serving.

8 ounces ground turkey or extra-lean ground beef
2 cups sliced fresh mushrooms
¾ cup chopped onion
½ cup chopped green or red sweet pepper
3 cloves garlic, minced
1 8-ounce can low-sodium tomato sauce
1 7½-ounce can tomatoes, cut up
1 6-ounce can low-sodium tomato paste
2 teaspoons dried Italian seasoning, crushed
6 packaged no-boil lasagna noodles (½ of an 8-ounce package of no-boil) or 6 regular lasagna noodles
1 beaten egg
1½ cups light or fat-free ricotta cheese
¼ cup grated Parmesan cheese
¼ teaspoon ground black pepper
Nonstick spray coating
½ cup shredded reduced-fat mozzarella cheese (2 ounces)
2 tablespoons grated Parmesan cheese
Fresh basil (optional)

● For meat sauce, in a large saucepan cook turkey or beef, mushrooms, onion, sweet pepper, and garlic until meat is no longer pink and vegetables are tender. Drain well.

● Stir in the tomato sauce, *undrained* tomatoes, tomato paste, and Italian seasoning. Bring to boiling; reduce heat. Cover and simmer for 15 minutes, stirring occasionally.

● Meanwhile, soak no-boil noodles in warm water for 10 minutes. (Or, cook regular noodles according to the package directions.) Drain well; set aside.

● For filling, in a medium bowl stir together the egg, ricotta cheese, the ¼ cup Parmesan cheese, and the black pepper.

● Spray a 2-quart rectangular baking dish with nonstick coating. Layer half of the noodles in dish, trimming to fit as necessary. Spread with half of the filling. Top with half of the meat sauce. Repeat layers. Sprinkle with mozzarella cheese and the 2 tablespoons Parmesan cheese. Cover loosely with foil. Bake in a 375° oven for 30 to 35 minutes or until heated through. Let stand for 10 minutes. If desired, garnish with fresh basil. Makes 6 to 8 servings.

TOTAL FAT: 11 g
DAILY VALUE FAT: 16%
SATURATED FAT: 5 g
DAILY VALUE SATURATED FAT: 25%

NUTRITION FACTS PER SERVING:

Calories	312
Total Fat	11 g
Saturated Fat	5 g
Cholesterol	84 mg
Sodium	335 mg
Carbohydrate	30 g
Fiber	4 g
Protein	26 g

EXCHANGES:
1 Starch
2 Vegetable
3 Medium-Fat Meat

PREPARATION TIME: 30 minutes
COOKING TIME: 35 minutes
STANDING TIME: 10 minutes

Garlic-Sage-Marinated Beef
Pot Roast

Surprised to see pot roast in an Italian cookbook? In Italy, pasture land is scarce and meat usually is prepared in small portions. Pot roast is considered a special-occasion dish.

1   2- to 2½-pound boneless beef chuck
    pot roast
¾ cup dry red wine or tomato juice
2   tablespoons tomato paste
1   tablespoon snipped fresh sage or
    ½ teaspoon ground sage
2   teaspoons instant beef bouillon granules
¼ teaspoon pepper
10 cloves garlic, halved
1   tablespoon cooking oil
1¼ pound whole tiny new potatoes
    or 4 medium potatoes
4   medium carrots, cut into 2-inch pieces
2   small onions, cut into wedges
2   stalks celery, bias-sliced into 1-inch
    pieces
¼ cup all-purpose flour
    Fresh sage (optional)

● Trim fat from roast; place meat in a heavy plastic bag set in a bowl. Combine the wine or tomato juice, tomato paste, sage, bouillon granules, pepper, and garlic. Pour over meat. Seal bag and marinate in refrigerator for 6 to 24 hours, turning occasionally. Lift meat from marinade, reserving marinade.

● In a kettle or pot, brown the roast on both sides in hot oil. Drain well. Pour reserved marinade over roast. Bring to boiling; reduce heat. Cover and simmer for 1 hour.

● Remove a narrow strip of peel from around the center of each new potato. (Or, peel and quarter each medium potato.) Add potatoes, carrots, onions, and celery to meat. Cover and simmer 45 to 60 minutes or until tender, adding some water if necessary. Transfer meat and vegetables to a serving platter; cover to keep warm while preparing gravy.

● For gravy, measure pan juices; skim fat. If necessary, add *water* to equal 1¾ cups liquid; return to pan. Combine flour and ½ cup *cold water*. Stir into juices. Cook and stir until thickened and bubbly. Cook and stir for 1 minute more. Season to taste with *salt* and *pepper*. Serve gravy with meat and vegetables. If desired, garnish with sage. Makes 8 servings.

TOTAL FAT: 8 g
DAILY VALUE FAT: 12%
SATURATED FAT: 3 g
DAILY VALUE SATURATED FAT: 15%

**NUTRITION FACTS
PER SERVING:**

Calories	321
Total Fat	8 g
Saturated Fat	3 g
Cholesterol	78 mg
Sodium	345 mg
Carbohydrate	28 g
Fiber	3 g
Protein	29 g

EXCHANGES:
1½ Starch
1 Vegetable
3 Lean Meat

PREPARATION TIME: 30 minutes
MARINATING TIME: 6 hours
COOKING TIME: 2 hours

TOTAL FAT: 8 g
DAILY VALUE FAT: 12%
SATURATED FAT: 3 g
DAILY VALUE SATURATED FAT: 15%

NUTRITION FACTS
PER SERVING:

Calories	414
Total Fat	8 g
Saturated Fat	3 g
Cholesterol	41 mg
Sodium	484 mg
Carbohydrate	63 g
Fiber	9 g
Protein	23 g

EXCHANGES:
3 Starch
2 Vegetable
2 Lean Meat

PREPARATION TIME: 40 minutes
COOKING TIME: 50 minutes

Tomato-Sauced Penne
With Meatballs

Bulgur, a steamed, dried, and crushed wheat product, helps keep these meatballs moist. Look for bulgur in the supermarket near the rice.

⅓ cup bulgur
   Nonstick spray coating
1½ cups sliced fresh mushrooms
½ cup chopped onion
½ cup chopped green sweet pepper
2 cloves garlic, minced
2 14½-ounce cans low-sodium tomatoes,
   cut up
1 teaspoon sugar
1 teaspoon dried Italian seasoning,
   crushed
3 tablespoons cold water
1 tablespoon cornstarch
1 slightly beaten egg white
¼ cup soft bread crumbs
2 tablespoons finely chopped onion
½ teaspoon fennel seed, crushed
¼ teaspoon salt
8 ounces very lean ground beef
8 ounces packaged dried penne or
   mostaccioli
   Grated Parmesan cheese (optional)
   Snipped fresh basil (optional)

● In a small saucepan bring ½ cup *water* to boiling. Add bulgur; reduce heat. Cover and cook over low heat about 7 minutes or until bulgur is almost tender and all of the liquid has been absorbed. Set aside.

● Meanwhile, for the sauce, spray an *unheated* 3-quart saucepan with nonstick coating. Preheat saucepan over medium heat. Add mushrooms, the ½ cup onion, the sweet pepper, and garlic. Cook and stir about 3 minutes or until the onion is tender. Stir in *undrained* tomatoes, sugar, Italian seasoning, and ½ teaspoon *salt*. Bring to boiling; reduce heat. Cover and simmer for 20 minutes. Combine 3 tablespoons water and the cornstarch. Add to sauce; cook and stir until thickened and bubbly. Cook and stir for 2 minutes more. Keep warm over very low heat.

● In a medium bowl stir together egg white, bread crumbs, the 2 tablespoons onion, fennel seed, and the salt. Add the beef and softened bulgur; mix well. Shape into 24 balls. Place meatballs in a shallow baking pan.

● Bake meatballs in a 375° oven 15 minutes or until juices run clear. Drain meatballs on paper towels. Add meatballs to sauce. Heat through.

● Meanwhile, cook pasta according to package directions. Drain well. Serve meatballs and sauce over hot pasta. If desired, sprinkle with Parmesan cheese and basil. Makes 4 servings.

Spaghetti with Italian Meatballs

We trimmed the fat in this dish simply by using lean ground beef and adding not a speck of fat to the sauce. Our slimmed-down version saves 10 grams of fat per serving compared to the more traditional dish.

½ cup soft bread crumbs
1 slightly beaten egg white
2 tablespoons finely chopped onion
1½ teaspoons dried Italian seasoning, crushed
¼ teaspoon fennel seed, crushed
⅛ teaspoon salt
⅛ teaspoon ground red pepper
8 ounces very lean ground beef
8 ounces packaged dried spaghetti
   Nonstick spray coating
2 cups sliced fresh mushrooms
⅔ cup chopped onion
4 cloves garlic, minced
1 28-ounce can crushed tomatoes
½ cup water
½ of a 6-ounce can (⅓ cup) low-sodium tomato paste
½ teaspoon sugar
¼ teaspoon ground black pepper
   Finely shredded Parmesan cheese (optional)

● For meatballs, in a medium mixing bowl stir together the bread crumbs, egg white, the 2 tablespoons onion, *¼ teaspoon* of the Italian seasoning, fennel seed, salt, and ground red pepper. Add ground beef; mix well. Shape into 16 meatballs. Place meatballs in a 2-quart square baking dish. Bake, uncovered, in a 375° oven about 20 minutes or until juices run clear. Drain.

● Meanwhile, cook pasta according to package directions. Drain well. For sauce, spray an unheated large saucepan with nonstick coating. Preheat saucepan over medium heat. Add the mushrooms, the ⅔ cup onion, and the garlic and cook for 3 to 4 minutes or until tender. Stir in crushed tomatoes, water, tomato paste, sugar, black pepper, and remaining Italian seasoning. Bring to boiling; reduce heat. Cover and simmer for 15 minutes. Gently stir cooked meatballs into sauce; heat through. To serve, spoon meatball mixture over hot pasta. If desired, sprinkle with Parmesan cheese. Makes 4 servings.

Making Meatballs

Here's a tip from our Test Kitchen to ensure that you'll have the correct number of meatballs, and that they'll be more or less of equal size: Shape the meatball mixture into a square or rectangle on a piece of waxed paper. Then with a large knife, cut the mixture into the number of meatballs called for in the recipe.

TOTAL FAT: 8 g
DAILY VALUE FAT: 12%
SATURATED FAT: 3 g
DAILY VALUE SATURATED FAT: 4%

NUTRITION FACTS
PER SERVING:

Calories	431
Total Fat	8 g
Saturated Fat	3 g
Cholesterol	41 mg
Sodium	474 mg
Carbohydrate	66 g
Fiber	6 g
Protein	24 g

EXCHANGES:
3 Starch
2 Vegetable
2 Lean Meat

PREPARATION TIME: 30 minutes
COOKING TIME: 40 minutes

TOTAL FAT: 8 g
DAILY VALUE FAT: 12%
SATURATED FAT: 3 g
DAILY VALUE SATURATED FAT: 15%

NUTRITION FACTS
PER SERVING:

Calories	447
Total Fat	8 g
Saturated Fat	3 g
Cholesterol	41 mg
Sodium	314 mg
Carbohydrate	64 g
Fiber	8 g
Protein	27 g

EXCHANGES:
3½ Starch
2 Vegetable
2 Lean Meat

PREPARATION TIME: 15 minutes
COOKING TIME: 45 minutes

Bolognese Meat Sauce
With Pasta

Traditionally, Bolognese (boh-luh-NEEZ) sauce is full of meat. We've cut back on fat and calories by substituting lentils for part of the meat.

2 tablespoons finely chopped pancetta (optional)
12 ounces extra-lean ground beef
2 14½-ounce cans low-sodium tomatoes, cut up
1 cup chopped onion
¾ cup dry lentils
¼ cup finely chopped carrot
¼ cup finely chopped celery
¼ cup snipped parsley
¼ cup tomato paste (⅓ of a 6-ounce can)
1 teaspoon instant beef bouillon granules
1 cup water
½ cup dry white wine or beef broth
12 ounces packaged dried pasta, such as penne, spaghetti, or mostaccioli
⅓ cup evaporated skim milk
Grated Parmesan cheese (optional)

● In a large saucepan or kettle cook pancetta (if using) just until crisp. Add ground beef; cook until meat is no longer pink. Drain well.

● If desired, pass *undrained* tomatoes through a food mill or sieve. Or, process in blender or food processor until nearly smooth. For meat sauce, add the tomatoes, onion, lentils, carrot, celery, parsley, tomato paste and bouillon granules to meat. Stir in the water and wine or broth. Bring to boiling; reduce heat. Cover and simmer about 40 minutes or until lentils are tender, stirring occasionally. Uncover and simmer about 5 minutes more or until of desired consistency.

● Cook pasta according to package directions. Drain well.

● Stir evaporated milk into meat mixture; heat through. Serve sauce over hot pasta. If desired, top with Parmesan cheese. Makes 6 servings.

Keeping Pasta Warm

What do you do when the pasta is done but the sauce has a few more minutes to cook? To keep the pasta warm without overcooking it, drain the pasta in a metal colander. Then place colander over a pot of boiling water. The steam from the water will keep the pasta warm and prevent it from drying out.

TOTAL FAT: 11 g
DAILY VALUE FAT: 16%
SATURATED FAT: 4 g
DAILY VALUE SATURATED FAT: 10%

NUTRITION FACTS
PER SERVING:

Calories	339
Total Fat	11 g
Saturated Fat	4 g
Cholesterol	59 mg
Sodium	349 mg
Carbohydrate	33 g
Fiber	3 g
Protein	24 g

EXCHANGES:
1½ Starch
1 Vegetable
2½ Medium-Fat Meat

PREPARATION TIME: 25 minutes
COOKING TIME: 20 minutes

Baked Cavatelli
With Meat Sauce

Large shells may be used in place of the cavatelli. Freeze the remaining tomato paste in an airtight container for another use.

8 ounces packaged dried cavatelli
1 14½-ounce can whole Italian-style tomatoes
½ of a 6-ounce can (⅓ cup) Italian-style tomato paste
¼ cup dry red wine or tomato juice
½ teaspoon sugar
½ teaspoon dried oregano, crushed or 2 teaspoons snipped fresh oregano
¼ teaspoon pepper
1 pound very lean ground beef
½ cup chopped onion
¼ cup sliced, pitted ripe olives
½ cup shredded part-skim mozzarella cheese (2 ounces)

● Cook pasta according to package directions. Drain pasta well.

● Meanwhile, in a blender container or food processor bowl combine *undrained* tomatoes, tomato paste, wine or tomato juice, sugar, dried oregano (if using), and pepper. Cover and blend or process until smooth. Set aside.

● In a large skillet cook ground beef and onion until meat is no longer pink. Drain well. Stir in tomato mixture. Bring to boiling; reduce heat. Cover and simmer for 10 minutes. Stir in pasta, fresh oregano (if using), and olives.

● Divide the pasta mixture among six 10- to 12-ounce individual casseroles. Bake, covered, in a 375° oven for 15 minutes. (Or, spoon all of the pasta mixture into a 2-quart casserole and bake, covered, for 30 minutes.) Sprinkle with mozzarella cheese. Bake, uncovered, 5 minutes more or until heated through. Makes 6 servings.

Beef Roll with Tomato Sauce

In Italy, this rolled, stuffed beef is known as braciola (brah-chee-OH-lah). For the lowest-fat dish, choose the top round steak over the flank steak—top round steak is the leaner of the two.

1 pound beef flank steak or top round
    steak, cut ½ inch thick
    Salt
⅓ cup grated Parmesan cheese
¼ cup golden raisins, snipped
¼ cup shredded carrot
¼ cup snipped parsley
3 tablespoons toasted pine nuts or slivered
    almonds, chopped
2 cloves garlic, minced
⅛ teaspoon pepper
1 tablespoon olive oil or cooking oil
1 cup chopped onion
1 clove garlic, minced
1 cup beef broth
½ cup dry red wine or beef broth
¼ cup tomato paste (⅓ of a 6-ounce can)
6 ounces packaged dried pasta (such as
    penne or ziti), cooked and drained

● Score steak on both sides by making shallow cuts at 1-inch intervals diagonally across steak in a diamond pattern.

● With a meat mallet, pound flank steak or round steak into a 12×8-inch rectangle, working from center to edges. Sprinkle lightly with salt. Set aside. In a bowl combine the cheese, snipped raisins, carrot, parsley, pine nuts or almonds, 2 cloves garlic, and the pepper.

● Spread the raisin mixture over the meat. Roll up the meat, jelly-roll style, beginning from a short side. Tie the meat in 3 or 4 places with 100-percent cotton string.

● In a large skillet brown meat on all sides in hot oil. Add onion and the 1 clove garlic; cook until onion is tender. Stir in 1 cup beef broth, wine or beef broth, and tomato paste. Heat to boiling; reduce heat. Cover and simmer about 45 minutes or until meat is tender. Remove meat from skillet. If necessary, boil sauce, uncovered, about 5 minutes to reduce to 1½ cups.

● Meanwhile, cook pasta according to package directions. Drain well. To serve, remove strings and slice meat into 6 or 12 slices. Arrange meat slices on hot pasta. Spoon sauce over top. Makes 6 servings.

TOTAL FAT: 12 g
DAILY VALUE FAT: 18%
SATURATED FAT: 4 g
DAILY VALUE SATURATED FAT: 20%

NUTRITION FACTS
PER SERVING:

Calories	328
Total Fat	12 g
Saturated Fat	4 g
Cholesterol	44 mg
Sodium	471 mg
Carbohydrate	30 g
Fiber	2 g
Protein	23 g

EXCHANGES:
1 Starch
1 Vegetable
2½ Lean Meat
½ Fruit
1 Fat

PREPARATION TIME: 40 minutes
COOKING TIME: 45 minutes

TOTAL FAT: 8 g
DAILY VALUE FAT: 12%
SATURATED FAT: 2 g
DAILY VALUE SATURATED FAT: 10%

NUTRITION FACTS
PER SERVING:

Calories	249
Total Fat	8 g
Saturated Fat	2 g
Cholesterol	61 mg
Sodium	496 mg
Carbohydrate	23 g
Fiber	1 g
Protein	19 g

EXCHANGES:
1 Starch
1 Vegetable
2 Lean Meat

PREPARATION TIME: 15 minutes
COOKING TIME: 1 hour

Osso Buco

We used several store-bought seasonings to simplify this variation of classic osso buco—braised veal shanks prepared with wine and tomatoes.

2 to 2½ pounds veal shanks, cut into 2½-inch pieces
  Lemon-pepper seasoning
  Salt
2 tablespoons all-purpose flour
2 tablespoons cooking oil
1 14½-ounce can tomatoes, cut up
1 cup chopped onion
½ cup water
¼ cup dry white wine or chicken broth
2 tablespoons mixed vegetable flakes
½ teaspoon instant beef bouillon granules
½ teaspoon dried Italian seasoning, crushed
¼ teaspoon dried finely shredded orange peel
⅛ teaspoon dried minced garlic
  Dash pepper
2 to 3 cups hot cooked rice
1 tablespoon snipped parsley or 1 teaspoon dried parsley flakes
½ cup shredded carrot (optional)

● Sprinkle veal with lemon-pepper seasoning and salt. Coat lightly with flour; shake off excess.

● In a kettle brown veal in hot oil. Drain well. Add the *undrained* tomatoes, onion, water, wine or broth, vegetable flakes, bouillon granules, Italian seasoning, orange peel, garlic, and pepper. Bring to boiling; reduce heat. Cover and simmer 50 to 60 minutes or until tender.

● Remove meat from kettle; cut meat from bones. Transfer meat to a serving platter. Cover and keep warm. Boil broth mixture gently, uncovered, about 10 minutes or until of desired consistency. To serve, toss rice with parsley and, if desired, shredded carrot. Place meat on rice. Spoon broth mixture over meat; pass remaining broth mixture. Makes 6 servings.

TOTAL FAT: 11 g
DAILY VALUE FAT: 16%
SATURATED FAT: 2 g
DAILY VALUE SATURATED FAT: 10%

NUTRITION FACTS
PER SERVING:

Calories	317
Total Fat	11 g
Saturated Fat	2 g
Cholesterol	100 mg
Sodium	333 mg
Carbohydrate	17 g
Fiber	3 g
Protein	32 g

EXCHANGES:
1 Starch
1 Vegetable
4 Lean Meat

PREPARATION TIME: 20 minutes
COOKING TIME: 15 minutes

Veal Scaloppine with Marsala

Marsala is a fortified wine from Sicily. The dry marsala in veal scaloppine provides the signature rich, smoky flavor.

3 cups fresh mushrooms (such as crimini, porcini, morel, portobello, shiitake, or button), quartered, halved, or sliced
½ cup sliced green onion
4 teaspoons olive oil or cooking oil
1 pound veal leg round steak or sirloin steak or 4 boneless, skinless chicken breast halves
¼ teaspoon salt
¼ teaspoon pepper
⅔ cup dry marsala or dry sherry
½ cup chicken broth
1 tablespoon snipped fresh sage or ½ teaspoon dried sage, crushed

● In a 12-inch skillet cook mushrooms and green onion in *2 teaspoons* of the hot oil for 4 to 5 minutes or until tender. Remove from skillet; set aside.

● Meanwhile, cut veal into 4 serving-size pieces. (If using chicken, rinse and pat dry with paper towels.) Place 1 piece of veal (or 1 chicken breast) between 2 sheets of plastic wrap. Working from the center to the edges, pound lightly with the flat side of a meat mallet to about ⅛-inch thickness. Remove wrap. Repeat with remaining veal or chicken.

● Sprinkle meat with the salt and pepper. In the same skillet cook *half* of the veal or chicken in remaining hot oil over medium-high heat about 1 minute on each side or until no longer pink. Transfer to warm dinner plates; keep warm. Repeat with remaining veal or chicken.

● Carefully add marsala or sherry and chicken broth to drippings in skillet. Bring to boiling; boil gently, uncovered, about 2 minutes or until cooking liquid measures ½ cup, scraping up any browned bits. Return mushroom mixture to skillet; add sage. Heat through.

● To serve, spoon the mushroom mixture over meat. Serve immediately. Makes 4 servings.

Veal Saltimbocca

It takes only one bite of these delicious veal rolls to know why they're called saltimbocca, or "jump in your mouth." Look for fresh sage leaves in the supermarket produce department.

12 ounces boneless veal leg top round steak
   or veal leg sirloin steak, cut ¼ inch
   thick, or 12 ounces boneless, skinless
   chicken breast halves
4 slices prosciutto (2 ounces), halved, or
   2 thin slices cooked ham, quartered
8 fresh sage leaves
2 teaspoons olive oil or cooking oil
   Dash pepper
⅓ cup dry white wine
2 tablespoons snipped parsley
2 tablespoons grated Parmesan cheese
2 cups hot cooked rice

● Rinse chicken (if using); pat dry with paper towels. Cut veal or chicken into 8 pieces. Place each piece of meat between two pieces of plastic wrap. Working from the center to the edges, pound the meat lightly with the flat side of a meat mallet to ⅛-inch thickness. Remove plastic wrap. Place a slice of prosciutto or ham on top of each piece of meat. Add a sage leaf; secure with a wooden pick.

● Pour the oil into a 12-inch skillet; heat over medium-high heat for 1 minute. Add the veal or chicken. Cook for 1 to 2 minutes on each side or until tender and no longer pink. Season with the pepper. Remove meat from skillet; cover and keep meat warm.

● Remove skillet from heat; let cool 1 minute. Carefully add the wine. Return skillet to heat; cook for 2 to 3 minutes or until wine is reduced slightly, scraping up browned bits in skillet. Add the pan juices, parsley, and Parmesan cheese to the rice; toss to combine. Remove wooden picks from meat. Serve meat on top of rice. Makes 4 servings.

TOTAL FAT: 11 g
DAILY VALUE FAT: 16%
SATURATED FAT: 2 g
DAILY VALUE SATURATED FAT: 10%

NUTRITION FACTS
PER SERVING:

Calories	333
Total Fat	11 g
Saturated Fat	2 g
Cholesterol	71 mg
Sodium	388 mg
Carbohydrate	27 g
Fiber	2 g
Protein	27 g

EXCHANGES:
2 Starch
3 Lean Meat

PREPARATION TIME: 20 minutes
COOKING TIME: 5 minutes

Creamy Green Beans
And Pasta

We flavor this dish with a small amount of the spicy Italian bacon called pancetta (pan-CHEH-tuh). Like bacon, it should be cooked before using. You can also substitute cooked lean ham.

8 ounces fresh green beans, cut into 1-inch pieces, or one 9-ounce package frozen cut green beans
6 ounces packaged dried bow-tie pasta, multicolored elbow macaroni, or gemelli pasta
1 cup sliced fresh mushrooms (such as shiitake, crimini, brown, or button)
¼ cup sliced green onion
1 8-ounce carton plain low-fat yogurt
2 tablespoons all-purpose flour
2 teaspoons prepared mustard
⅛ teaspoon ground nutmeg
⅛ teaspoon pepper
¼ cup finely chopped cooked pancetta or ham (2 ounces)
¼ cup grated Parmesan cheese

● If using fresh green beans, cook in a covered saucepan in a small amount of *boiling water* for 20 to 25 minutes or until crisp-tender. Drain.

● Meanwhile, in a large saucepan cook pasta according to package directions, adding the mushrooms, frozen green beans (if using), and green onion during the last 4 to 5 minutes of cooking. Drain pasta and vegetables in a colander. Set pasta mixture aside.

● For sauce, in the same large saucepan stir together yogurt, flour, mustard, nutmeg, and pepper. Cook and stir until thickened and bubbly. Stir in pasta mixture, cooked fresh green beans (if using), and pancetta or ham. Heat through. To serve, sprinkle with Parmesan cheese. Makes 4 servings.

99
Main Dishes

TOTAL FAT: 5 g
DAILY VALUE FAT: 7%
SATURATED FAT: 2 g
DAILY VALUE SATURATED FAT: 10%

NUTRITION FACTS PER SERVING:

Calories	292
Total Fat	5 g
Saturated Fat	2 g
Cholesterol	14 mg
Sodium	335 mg
Carbohydrate	48 g
Fiber	4 g
Protein	16 g

EXCHANGES:
2 Starch
2 Vegetable
1 Medium-Fat Meat
¼ Milk

START TO FINISH: 40 minutes

TOTAL FAT: 4 g

DAILY VALUE FAT: 6%

SATURATED FAT: 1 g

DAILY VALUE SATURATED FAT: 5%

NUTRITION FACTS
PER SERVING:

Calories	179
Total Fat	4 g
Saturated Fat	1 g
Cholesterol	50 mg
Sodium	193 mg
Carbohydrate	16 g
Fiber	5 g
Protein	20 g

EXCHANGES:
3 Vegetable
2 Lean Meat

PREPARATION TIME: 10 minutes

MARINATING TIME: 30 minutes

COOKING TIME: 35 minutes

Pork with Fennel and Carrots

Pork tenderloin fits into a healthful diet because it is extremely lean, with only 4 grams of fat per 3-ounce serving. If you're lucky enough to find fresh baby carrots, use them to make this dish extra special.

12 ounces pork tenderloin
⅔ cup orange juice
⅓ cup water
2 tablespoons thinly sliced green onion
1 tablespoon snipped fresh sage
     or ½ teaspoon ground sage
1 tablespoon Dijon-style mustard
1 teaspoon fennel seed, crushed
2 small fennel bulbs (1¼ to 1½ pounds)
1 cup packaged, peeled baby carrots
2 teaspoons cornstarch

● Trim any fat from meat. Place the tenderloin in a large plastic bag set inside a bowl. Stir together the orange juice, water, green onion, sage, mustard, and fennel seed. Pour over meat in bag. Seal bag. Marinate for 30 minutes at room temperature or 4 hours in refrigerator.

● Meanwhile, cut off and discard upper stalks of fennel bulbs, including feathery leaves (reserve leaves for garnish, if desired). Remove any wilted outer layers of stalks; cut off a thin slice from base. Wash. Cut fennel lengthwise into quarters. Cook fennel quarters and baby carrots in a covered saucepan in a small amount of *boiling water* about 10 minutes or until nearly tender. Drain and set aside.

● Remove tenderloin from marinade. Reserve *1 cup* marinade. (If necessary, add water to make 1 cup liquid.) Pat meat dry with paper towels. Place tenderloin on a rack in a shallow roasting pan. Insert a meat thermometer in center of tenderloin. Roast, uncovered, in a 425° oven for 15 minutes. Add cooked fennel and carrots to roasting pan. Roast 10 to 20 minutes more or until thermometer registers 160°. Cover meat with foil and let stand 5 minutes before carving.

● Meanwhile, for sauce, in a small saucepan stir together reserved marinade and the cornstarch. Cook and stir over medium heat until thickened and bubbly. Cook and stir 2 minutes more. Remove from heat.

● To serve, slice roast. Serve with fennel and carrots. Spoon sauce over meat and vegetables. If desired, garnish with reserved fennel leaves. Makes 4 servings.

Braised Pork in Milk

This simple dish is popular throughout Italy. Although garlic cloves are not traditionally used, they add a mild, delicious flavor to the meat.

1   1½- to 1¾-pound boneless pork loin
      roast (single loin)
3   medium leeks or 1 large onion, thinly
      sliced
1   small bulb garlic, peeled (8 cloves)
1   tablespoon cooking oil
3   cups milk
¼   teaspoon salt
⅛   teaspoon pepper
¼   cup cold water
3   tablespoons all-purpose flour
6   ounces packaged dried spinach
      fettuccine

● Trim fat from pork roast. In an oven-safe pot cook leeks and whole garlic cloves in hot oil until leeks are tender and begin to brown. Push leeks and garlic to the side of pot. Add roast to pan. Brown well on all sides.

● Add the milk, salt, and pepper to pot. Bake, covered, in a 400° oven for about 45 minutes or until tender.

● Transfer roast to a warm serving platter. For sauce, strain pan juices. Skim off any fat. Reserve 2 cups of the cooking liquid and return to pot. Gradually stir cold water into flour. Stir into cooking liquid. Cook and stir until thickened and bubbly. Cook and stir 1 minute more. To serve, slice meat and serve with fettuccine and sauce. Makes 6 servings.

Go Whole Hog

Many health conscious cooks are surprised to learn that pork can be part of a healthful diet. Today's pork comes from a leaner hog, and its visible fat is more closely trimmed. A 3-ounce portion of pork loin (trimmed of fat) has about 170 calories and 7 grams of fat.

TOTAL FAT: 13 g
DAILY VALUE FAT: 19%
SATURATED FAT: 5 g
DAILY VALUE SATURATED FAT: 25%

NUTRITION FACTS
PER SERVING:

Calories	367
Total Fat	13 g
Saturated Fat	5 g
Cholesterol	76 mg
Sodium	218 mg
Carbohydrate	30 g
Fiber	2 g
Protein	32 g

EXCHANGES:
1½ Starch
3 Lean Meat
½ Milk
½ Fat

PREPARATION TIME: 15 minutes
COOKING TIME: 55 minutes

TOTAL FAT: 9 g
DAILY VALUE FAT: 13%
SATURATED FAT: 3 g
DAILY VALUE SATURATED FAT: 15%

NUTRITION FACTS
PER SERVING:

Calories	222
Total Fat	9 g
Saturated Fat	3 g
Cholesterol	69 mg
Sodium	142 mg
Carbohydrate	9 g
Fiber	1 g
Protein	25 g

EXCHANGES:
½ **Fruit**
3½ **Lean Meat**

PREPARATION TIME: 15 minutes
COOKING TIME: 1 hour and
10 minutes

Italian Pork Roast

Fresh pork is light pink in color. When this roast reaches the desired 160° internal temperature, the meat will be slightly pink, but when a small cut is made in the meat, the juices should run clear.

2　teaspoons snipped fresh rosemary
　　or 1 teaspoon dried rosemary, crushed
1　clove garlic, minced
1　teaspoon olive oil or cooking oil
1　1½- to 2-pound boneless pork top loin
　　roast (single loin)
1　cup apple juice
⅓　cup sliced leek (1 medium) or chopped
　　onion
1　small Golden Delicious or Granny Smith
　　apple, cored and chopped
2　teaspoons cornstarch
2　tablespoons white wine vinegar
¼　teaspoon salt
⅛　teaspoon pepper

● In a small bowl combine rosemary, garlic, and olive oil. Rub evenly over the roast. Place the prepared roast on a rack in a shallow roasting pan. Insert a meat thermometer in center of roast. Roast, uncovered, in a 325° oven for 1 to 1½ hours or until the thermometer registers 160°. Transfer roast to a warm serving platter. Keep roast warm. Reserve *2 tablespoons* of the pan drippings.

● In a medium saucepan bring *¾ cup* of the apple juice to boiling. Add leek and apple; reduce heat. Cover and simmer for 4 minutes or just until tender. Stir together remaining ¼ cup apple juice and the cornstarch. Stir into leek mixture. Stir in reserved pan drippings, vinegar, salt, and pepper. Cook and stir until thickened and bubbly. Cook and stir for 2 minutes more.

● To serve, cut roast into slices and pass sauce with roast. Makes 6 to 8 servings.

Prosciutto, Spinach, and
Pasta Casserole

Prosciutto (proh-SHOO-toh) is a spicy, cured ham, originally made in Italy. You can substitute cooked lean ham if you like.

8 ounces packaged dried orecchiette, mostaccioli, or ziti
1 tablespoon margarine or butter
2 medium onions, cut into thin wedges, or 5 medium leeks, sliced
2 cloves garlic, minced
¼ cup all-purpose flour
½ teaspoon aniseed, crushed
1¾ cups skim milk
1½ cups reduced-sodium chicken broth
¼ cup grated Parmesan cheese
1 10-ounce package frozen chopped spinach, thawed and well drained
2 ounces prosciutto, cut into thin bite-size strips
1 medium tomato, seeded and chopped

● Cook the pasta according to the package directions. Drain pasta; rinse pasta with cold water. Drain again.

● In a large saucepan melt margarine or butter. Add onions or leeks and garlic. Cover and cook about 5 minutes or until onions are tender, stirring occasionally. Stir in flour and aniseed. Add the milk and chicken broth all at once. Cook and stir until thickened and bubbly. Stir in Parmesan cheese. Stir in the cooked pasta, spinach, and prosciutto. Spoon the mixture into a 2-quart casserole.

● Cover and bake in a 350° oven for 25 to 30 minutes or until heated through. Let stand about 5 minutes. To serve, stir gently and top with chopped tomato. Makes 6 servings.

Sweet Aniseed

A member of the parsley family, this plant has been around for centuries. The leaves and the seed both have a wonderful sweet licorice taste. Aniseed may be used in sweet as well as savory dishes and lends its flavor to some liqueurs, such as annisette. It gives this dish an interesting flavor—don't be tempted to skip it. You'll find aniseed at the supermarket next to other herbs and spices.

TOTAL FAT: 5 g
DAILY VALUE FAT: 7%
SATURATED FAT: 2 g
DAILY VALUE SATURATED FAT: 10%

NUTRITION FACTS
PER SERVING:

Calories	262
Total Fat	5 g
Saturated Fat	2 g
Cholesterol	9 mg
Sodium	415 mg
Carbohydrate	42 g
Fiber	3 g
Protein	13 g

EXCHANGES:
2½ Starch
1 Vegetable
½ Lean Meat
½ Fat

PREPARATION TIME: 25 minutes
COOKING TIME: 25 minutes

Grilled Tuna
With Tuscan Beans

*Tuna and beans—*tonno e fagioli—*is a favorite combination in Italian coastal towns. Using canned beans makes our version fast and easy.*

1 **pound fresh or frozen tuna, swordfish, halibut, shark, or salmon steaks**
2 **cloves garlic, minced**
1 **tablespoon olive oil**
1 **14½-ounce can Italian-style stewed tomatoes, cut up**
2 **teaspoons snipped fresh sage or**
  ¼ teaspoon ground sage
1 **15-ounce can small white beans, rinsed and drained**
2 **teaspoons olive oil**
2 **teaspoons lemon juice**
⅛ **teaspoon pepper**
  Nonstick spray coating
  Fresh sage (optional)

● Thaw fish, if frozen. For grilling, preheat coals to medium-hot while preparing beans and fish.

● For beans, in a medium skillet cook the garlic in 1 tablespoon hot oil for 15 seconds. Stir in the *undrained* tomatoes and the 2 teaspoons sage. Bring to boiling; reduce heat. Simmer, uncovered, for 5 minutes. Stir in beans; heat through.

● Meanwhile, rinse fish; pat dry with paper towels. Measure thickness of fish. Cut fish into 4 serving-size portions. Brush both sides of fish with the 2 teaspoons oil and the lemon juice; sprinkle with the pepper.

● To grill, spray an unheated grill rack or grill basket with nonstick coating. Place fish steaks on grill rack or in grill basket. Grill on an uncovered grill directly over coals until fish flakes easily when tested with a fork (allow 4 to 6 minutes per each ½-inch thickness). If the fish is more than 1 inch thick, gently turn it halfway through grilling. (Or, to broil fish, place on the greased unheated rack of a broiler pan. Broil 4 inches from the heat for 4 to 6 minutes per ½ inch of thickness. If the fish is more than 1 inch thick, gently turn it halfway through broiling.)

● To serve, remove the skin from fish. Spoon beans on each serving plate and top with fish. If desired, garnish with sage. Makes 4 servings.

TOTAL FAT: 7 g
DAILY VALUE FAT: 10%
SATURATED FAT: 1 g
DAILY VALUE SATURATED FAT: 5%

NUTRITION FACTS
PER SERVING:

Calories	298
Total Fat	7 g
Saturated Fat	1 g
Cholesterol	49 mg
Sodium	536 mg
Carbohydrate	25 g
Fiber	5 g
Protein	33 g

EXCHANGES:
1½ **Starch**
1 **Vegetable**
3 **Very Lean Meat**
½ **Fat**

PREPARATION TIME: 15 minutes
COOKING TIME: Depends on thickness of fish

TOTAL FAT: 3 g

DAILY VALUE FAT: 4%

SATURATED FAT: 1 g

DAILY VALUE SATURATED FAT: 5%

NUTRITION FACTS

PER SERVING:

Calories	154
Total Fat	3 g
Saturated Fat	1 g
Cholesterol	54 mg
Sodium	195 mg
Carbohydrate	8 g
Fiber	2 g
Protein	23 g

EXCHANGES:

1½ Vegetable

3 Very Lean Meat

PREPARATION TIME: 15 minutes

COOKING TIMES: 20 minutes for sauce; fish depends on thickness

Fish Fillets
With Red Pepper Sauce

The Italian "boot" is made up of almost 2,700 miles of coastline, so it's no wonder Italians enjoy the freshest of fish. Use these tips when you choose fresh fish: Make sure the fish in the counter is displayed on a bed of ice. The fish should have a mild smell, not a strong fishy odor. Avoid fish that is dry around the edges.

3	medium red sweet peppers, chopped, or one 12-ounce jar roasted red sweet peppers, drained and chopped

2	cloves garlic, minced

2	teaspoons olive oil

½	cup water

⅓	cup loosely packed fresh snipped basil or 1 teaspoon dried basil, crushed

2	tablespoons tomato paste

1	tablespoon red wine vinegar

½	teaspoon sugar

⅛	teaspoon salt
	Dash ground black pepper

1	pound fresh or frozen fish fillets

¼	cup water

1	lemon, sliced
	Fresh basil (optional)

● For sauce, in a large skillet cook fresh sweet peppers and garlic in hot oil over medium heat about 20 minutes, stirring occasionally. (Or, if using peppers from a jar, in a 2-quart saucepan cook garlic in oil for 30 to 60 seconds or until light brown. Stir in peppers; remove from heat.)

● Place the pepper-garlic mixture in a blender container or food processor bowl. Cover; blend or process until nearly smooth. Add the ½ cup water, the basil, tomato paste, vinegar, sugar, salt, and black pepper. Cover and blend or process with several on-off turns until basil is just chopped and mixture is nearly smooth. Transfer to a 1-quart saucepan. Cook and stir sauce over medium heat until heated through.

● Meanwhile, measure thickness of fish. In a large skillet bring the ¼ cup water and *half* of the lemon slices just to boiling. Carefully add fish. Return just to boiling; reduce heat. Cover and simmer until fish flakes easily when tested with a fork. (Allow 4 to 6 minutes per ½-inch thickness for fresh fish; 6 to 9 minutes per ½-inch thickness for frozen fish.) Remove fish from skillet.

● To serve, spoon some of the sauce onto 4 dinner plates. Place a fillet on top of sauce on each plate. Garnish with remaining lemon slices and, if desired, basil. Freeze any remaining sauce for another time. Makes 4 servings.

Lemon-Thyme Fish Kabobs

Leave at least ¼ inch of space between kabob pieces to ensure even cooking and eliminate the raw areas that can occur when foods are crowded together.

12 ounces fresh or frozen skinless swordfish, tuna, or shark steaks, cut 1 inch thick
¼ cup lemon juice
1 tablespoon olive oil
½ teaspoon dried thyme, crushed
½ teaspoon salt
⅛ teaspoon pepper
12 medium, fresh mushrooms
2 small zucchini or yellow summer squash, cut into 1-inch slices
1 medium yellow, green, or red sweet pepper, cut into 1-inch pieces
8 cherry tomatoes
3 cups hot cooked rice or orzo (rosamarina)

● Thaw fish, if frozen. Cut fish into 1-inch cubes. Place fish in a medium bowl. Add lemon juice, oil, thyme, salt, and pepper, tossing to coat. Let stand at room temperature for 30 minutes. Drain, reserving marinade.

● Alternately thread the fish cubes, mushrooms, zucchini or summer squash, and sweet pepper onto eight 12-inch skewers, leaving about ¼ inch between pieces.

● Place the kabobs on a lightly greased unheated rack of a broiler pan. Brush the kabobs with reserved marinade. Broil 4 inches from the heat for 6 minutes. Turn kabobs over. Broil for 4 to 6 minutes more or until fish flakes easily when tested with a fork, placing a cherry tomato on the end of each the last 2 minutes of broiling. (Or, to grill, place kabobs on a greased grill rack; grill, uncovered, directly over *medium-hot* coals for 8 to 12 minutes, turning once and placing the tomatoes on the ends of skewers during the last 2 minutes of grilling.) Serve with hot cooked rice or orzo. Makes 4 servings.

Fish: A Prize Catch

Although fish and seafood contain cholesterol and saturated fat, it's generally a lot less than meat or even poultry. Fish can, and should, be enjoyed in a healthful diet. Fish and shellfish contain a type of unsaturated fat, called omega-3 fatty acids, which has been shown to be kind to your heart. But be sure to eat the real thing. Fish oil pills are high in fat and calories, and their long-term effects are unknown.

TOTAL FAT: 7 g
DAILY VALUE FAT: 10%
SATURATED FAT: 1 g
DAILY VALUE SATURATED FAT: 5%

NUTRITION FACTS PER SERVING:

Calories	348
Total Fat	7 g
Saturated Fat	1 g
Cholesterol	23 mg
Sodium	327 mg
Carbohydrate	55 g
Fiber	4 g
Protein	18 g

EXCHANGES:
3 Starch
2 Vegetable
1½ Very Lean Meat
1 Fat

PREPARATION TIME: 25 minutes
MARINATING TIME: 30 minutes
COOKING TIME: 10 minutes

TOTAL FAT: 7 g
DAILY VALUE FAT: 10%
SATURATED FAT: 2 g
DAILY VALUE SATURATED FAT: 10%

**NUTRITION FACTS
PER SERVING:**

Calories	357
Total Fat	7 g
Saturated Fat	2 g
Cholesterol	126 mg
Sodium	397 mg
Carbohydrate	49 g
Fiber	6 g
Protein	24 g

EXCHANGES:
2½ Starch
2 Very Lean Meat
2 Vegetable
½ Fat

**PREPARATION TIME: 30 minutes
COOKING TIME: 45 minutes**

Linguine with Garlic Shrimp

No need to fear the amount of garlic in this delicious dish since it's roasted to a mellow, buttery paste. It has many uses—spread it on Italian bread, stir it into mashed potatoes, or add it to mayonnaise for sandwiches.

12 ounces fresh or frozen, peeled, deveined shrimp
2 large bulbs garlic
8 ounces packaged dried regular and/or spinach linguine or fettuccine
2 cups sliced fresh mushrooms
¾ cup chopped yellow or green sweet pepper (1 medium)
1 tablespoon olive oil or cooking oil
½ cup water
1 tablespoon snipped fresh basil
   or 1 teaspoon dried basil, crushed
2 teaspoons cornstarch
1½ teaspoons snipped fresh oregano
   or ½ teaspoon dried oregano, crushed
½ teaspoon instant chicken bouillon granules
⅛ teaspoon ground black pepper
2 medium tomatoes, peeled, seeded, and chopped
¼ cup finely shredded Parmesan cheese

● Thaw shrimp, if frozen. Set aside.

● For garlic paste, cut ½ inch off the pointed top portions of garlic bulbs. Remove the outer papery layers of the garlic. Place both bulbs on a square piece of foil. Bring edges of foil together to form a pouch. Seal. Bake garlic in a 375° oven for 35 to 40 minutes or until very soft. When cool enough to handle, use your fingers to press garlic pulp from each clove. Mash pulp with a spoon or fork to make a smooth paste (should have about 2 to 3 tablespoons). Set aside.

● Cook pasta according to package directions. Drain. Cover to keep warm.

● Meanwhile, in a large saucepan cook mushrooms and sweet pepper in hot oil until pepper is tender.

● In a small bowl stir together the garlic paste, water, basil, cornstarch, oregano, bouillon granules, and black pepper. Add to mushroom mixture in saucepan. Cook and stir until thickened and bubbly. Add the shrimp to the mushroom mixture. Cover and simmer about 2 minutes or until shrimp turn pink. Stir in tomatoes; heat through.

● To serve, spoon shrimp over pasta. Sprinkle with Parmesan cheese. Toss to combine. Makes 4 servings.

Crab and Fennel Risotto

Fennel is a celerylike vegetable that has a delicate licorice flavor. The seed from the fennel plant is a spice traditionally used in Italian sausage.

2 fennel bulbs with tops
1 cup sliced fresh mushrooms, such as shiitake, porcini, or button
½ teaspoon fennel seed, crushed
1 tablespoon olive oil
1 cup Arborio or medium-grain rice
3¼ cups water
1 teaspoon chicken bouillon granules
⅛ teaspoon pepper
1 cup cooked crabmeat; one 7-ounce can crabmeat, drained, flaked, and cartilage removed; or one 6-ounce package frozen crabmeat, thawed and drained
½ cup asparagus,* cut into 1-inch pieces
⅓ cup thinly sliced green onion
Fennel tops (optional)

● Trim fennel bulbs, reserving tops. Quarter bulbs lengthwise and slice. Measure 1 cup sliced fennel. Snip enough of the fennel tops to get 1 tablespoon; set aside. In a large saucepan cook mushrooms, the 1 cup fennel, and fennel seed in hot oil until tender. Stir in uncooked rice. Cook and stir over medium heat for 2 minutes more.

● Carefully stir in water, bouillon granules, and pepper. Bring to boiling; reduce heat. Cover and simmer for 20 minutes (do not lift cover).

● Remove saucepan from heat. Stir in crabmeat, asparagus, and green onion. Let stand, covered, for 5 minutes. (The rice should be tender but slightly firm, and the mixture should be creamy. If necessary, stir in a little water to reach the desired consistency.)

● Stir in snipped fennel tops. If desired, garnish with additional fennel tops. Makes 4 servings.

***Note:** If using thick asparagus spears, halve spears lengthwise, cut into 1-inch pieces, and cook in a small amount of *boiling water* until crisp-tender. Add to risotto.

TOTAL FAT: 5 g
DAILY VALUE FAT: 7%
SATURATED FAT: 1 g
DAILY VALUE SATURATED FAT: 5%

NUTRITION FACTS
PER SERVING:

Calories	307
Total Fat	5 g
Saturated Fat	1 g
Cholesterol	22 mg
Sodium	401 mg
Carbohydrate	54 g
Fiber	6 g
Protein	13 g

EXCHANGES:
2½ Starch
½ Lean Meat
2½ Vegetable
½ Fat

PREPARATION TIME: 10 minutes
COOKING TIME: 30 minutes

TOTAL FAT: 5 g

DAILY VALUE FAT: 7%

SATURATED FAT: 1 g

DAILY VALUE SATURATED FAT: 5%

NUTRITION FACTS

PER SERVING:

Calories	404
Total Fat	5 g
Saturated Fat	1 g
Cholesterol	34 mg
Sodium	377 mg
Carbohydrate	63 g
Fiber	4 g
Protein	24 g

EXCHANGES:

4 Starch

1 Vegetable

2 Lean Meat

START TO FINISH: 22 minutes

White Clam Sauce
With Spaghetti

Italians generally do not top seafood sauces with grated cheese. For added texture, sprinkle on some toasted bread crumbs instead.

8 ounces packaged dried spaghetti,
  linguine, or twisted spaghetti

2 6½-ounce cans minced clams

½ cup chopped onion

2 cloves garlic, minced

2 teaspoons olive oil

¾ cup skim milk

⅓ cup all-purpose flour

¼ teaspoon salt

¼ teaspoon lemon-pepper seasoning

½ cup frozen peas

¼ cup snipped parsley

¼ cup dry white wine or chicken broth

1 tablespoon snipped fresh basil or
  ½ teaspoon dried basil, crushed

  Grated Parmesan cheese or toasted bread
  crumbs (optional)

● Cook pasta according to package directions.

● Meanwhile, drain clams, reserving the liquid. Set clams aside. Add *water,* if necessary, to the reserved liquid to equal 1 cup. Set aside.

● For sauce, in a medium saucepan cook the onion and garlic in hot oil until onion is tender. In a screw-top jar shake together milk and flour until smooth. Add to saucepan along with salt, lemon-pepper seasoning, and the clam liquid. Cook and stir over medium heat until thickened and bubbly. Cook and stir for 1 minute more. Stir in the clams, peas, parsley, wine or broth, and basil. Heat through.

● Serve sauce over hot pasta. If desired, sprinkle each serving with Parmesan cheese or bread crumbs. Makes 4 servings.

Shrimp Fettuccine
With Wine Sauce

Shrimp is higher in cholesterol than other shellfish, but it is extremely low in fat. The 3 ounces of shrimp in each serving of this dish contribute only 1½ grams of fat.

12 ounces fresh or frozen, peeled, deveined shrimp
 6 ounces packaged dried spinach fettuccine and/or plain fettuccine, cooked
 2 cups sliced fresh mushrooms
 1 cup chopped onion
 2 cloves garlic, minced
 1 tablespoon olive oil or cooking oil
 ¼ cup dry white wine or water
 1 tablespoon snipped fresh basil
1½ teaspoons snipped fresh oregano
 1 teaspoon instant chicken bouillon granules
 1 teaspoon cornstarch
 ⅛ teaspoon pepper
 2 medium tomatoes, peeled, seeded, and chopped
 ¼ cup snipped parsley
 ¼ cup grated Parmesan cheese

● Thaw shrimp, if frozen.

● Cook pasta according to package directions.

● Meanwhile, in a large saucepan cook the mushrooms, onion, and garlic in hot oil until onion is tender. Combine the wine or water, basil, oregano, bouillon granules, cornstarch, and pepper. Add to saucepan. Cook and stir until bubbly.

● Add shrimp to wine mixture. Cover and simmer about 3 minutes or until shrimp turn pink. Stir in tomatoes and heat through. To serve, toss pasta with parsley. Spoon shrimp mixture over pasta. Sprinkle with Parmesan cheese. Makes 4 servings.

TOTAL FAT: 7 g
DAILY VALUE FAT: 10%
SATURATED FAT: 2 g
DAILY VALUE SATURATED FAT: 10%

NUTRITION FACTS
PER SERVING:

Calories	329
Total Fat	7 g
Saturated Fat	2 g
Cholesterol	135 mg
Sodium	493 mg
Carbohydrate	41 g
Fiber	3 g
Protein	23 g

EXCHANGES:
2 Starch
2 Vegetable
1½ Very Lean Meat
1 Fat

PREPARATION TIME: 18 minutes
COOKING TIME: 15 minutes

Shrimp-Artichoke Frittata

In Italy, frittatas—or Italian omelets—often are eaten in sandwiches or as a quick supper. Our version uses an egg substitute, skim milk, and a nonstick skillet to keep fat and cholesterol low.

4 ounces fresh or frozen shrimp in shells, peeled and deveined
½ of a 9-ounce package frozen artichoke hearts
1½ cups refrigerated or frozen egg product, thawed
¼ cup skim milk
¼ cup thinly sliced green onion
⅛ teaspoon garlic powder
⅛ teaspoon pepper
  Nonstick spray coating
3 tablespoons finely shredded Parmesan cheese

● Thaw shrimp, if frozen. Halve shrimp lengthwise; set aside. Cook artichokes according to package directions. Drain; cut artichoke hearts into quarters and set aside.

● In a medium bowl stir together the egg product, milk, green onion, garlic powder, and pepper; set aside.

● Spray an *unheated* large skillet with nonstick coating. Heat skillet over medium-high heat. Add shrimp and cook for 1 to 3 minutes or until pink.

● Add the egg mixture to skillet. Cook over medium-low heat. As the egg mixture sets, run a spatula around the edge of the skillet, lifting egg mixture to allow uncooked portion to flow underneath. Continue cooking and lifting edges until mixture is almost set (surface will be moist).

● Remove skillet from heat; distribute artichoke pieces evenly over the top. Sprinkle with the Parmesan cheese. Cover and let stand for 3 to 4 minutes or until top is set. Loosen bottom of frittata with a spatula. To serve, cut into wedges. Makes 4 servings.

TOTAL FAT: 1 g

DAILY VALUE FAT: 2%

SATURATED FAT: 0 g

DAILY VALUE SATURATED FAT: 0%

NUTRITION FACTS
PER SERVING:

Calories	199
Total Fat	1 g
Saturated Fat	0 g
Cholesterol	161 mg
Sodium	322 mg
Carbohydrate	24 g
Fiber	2 g
Protein	21 g

EXCHANGES:
1 Starch
1 Vegetable
2 Very Lean Meat

PREPARATION TIME: 20 minutes
COOKING TIME: 10 minutes

Shrimp with Peppers

For maximum eye appeal, use a mixture of green, red, and yellow sweet peppers. You can serve the shrimp over rice in place of orzo, if you wish.

1   **pound fresh or frozen shrimp, peeled and deveined**
1½ **cups chopped green, red, and/or yellow sweet peppers**
1   **cup chopped onion**
2   **teaspoons cornstarch**
2   **tablespoons dry marsala, dry white wine, or chicken broth**
½   **teaspoon finely shredded lemon peel**
2   **tablespoons lemon juice**
1   **teaspoon dried basil, crushed**
¼   **teaspoon salt**
⅛   **teaspoon crushed red pepper**
2   **cups hot cooked orzo**
    Lemon slices

● Thaw shrimp, if frozen. In a large skillet cook sweet peppers and onion covered in small amount of boiling *water* until tender (about 3 minutes). Drain. Toss shrimp with cornstarch.

● Stir shrimp, marsala, lemon peel, lemon juice, basil, salt, and crushed red pepper into the skillet. Cover and let cook over medium heat for 4 to 6 minutes or until shrimp turn pink, stirring occasionally. Serve with hot cooked orzo. Garnish with lemon slices. Makes 4 servings.

Selecting Shrimp

Shrimp are sold by the pound. The price per pound usually is determined by size—the bigger the shrimp, the higher the price and the fewer per pound. Fresh shrimp should be moist and firm, have translucent flesh, and smell fresh. Signs of poor quality are an ammonia smell and blackened edges or spots on the shells.

Eggplant Parmigiana

Traditional eggplant parmigiana is loaded with fat and calories, but this version has only 212 calories and 6 grams of fat per serving. We kept the flavor by parboiling the eggplant and zucchini instead of frying them and by using reduced-fat cheeses.

1   medium eggplant (1 pound)
2   cups bias-sliced zucchini (¼ inch thick)
¼   teaspoon salt
1   cup low-fat ricotta cheese or cottage
      cheese, drained
1   15-ounce container refrigerated light
      tomato pasta sauce with basil
      or 2 cups purchased light spaghetti
      sauce
1   small tomato, thinly sliced
½   cup shredded reduced-fat mozzarella
      cheese (2 ounces)
2   tablespoons grated Parmesan cheese

● If desired, peel the eggplant. Cut into ½-inch slices; halve each slice. In a kettle cook the eggplant, zucchini, and salt in a small amount of *boiling water* for 4 minutes. Drain; pat dry with paper towels.

● Divide the eggplant and zucchini among 4 individual au gratin dishes or casseroles. Top with ricotta cheese and tomato pasta sauce or spaghetti sauce. Top with the sliced tomato. Sprinkle with the mozzarella and Parmesan cheeses. Bake, uncovered, in a 350° oven for 20 to 25 minutes or until heated through. Makes 4 servings.

Sassy Sauces

If you're worried about pasta being "fattening," don't be. Pasta is a complex carbohydrate that by itself is low in fat. Of course, the fat and calories can easily add up when you top it with high-fat sauces. To control the fat and calories of a pasta dish, fix a tomato- or vegetable-based sauce, rather than a cream-based sauce. Most tomato sauces range from 0 to 7 grams fat per ½ cup. Compare that to a traditional Alfredo sauce, which has 25 to 44 grams fat per ½ cup. When selecting a ready-to-heat sauce, read and compare labels, paying attention to the fat and sodium content. Look for sauces labeled "low-fat" or "reduced-fat."

TOTAL FAT: 6 g
DAILY VALUE FAT: 9%
SATURATED FAT: 3 g
DAILY VALUE SATURATED FAT: 15%

NUTRITION FACTS
PER SERVING:

Calories	212
Total Fat	6 g
Saturated Fat	3 g
Cholesterol	21 mg
Sodium	560 mg
Carbohydrate	27 g
Fiber	6 g
Protein	15 g

EXCHANGES:
1 Starch
2 Vegetable
1 Medium-Fat Meat

PREPARATION TIME: 25 minutes
COOKING TIME: 20 minutes

Polenta with Two Sauces

Polenta is a cornmeal mush that Northern Italians eat in place of pasta. Serve polenta right from the pot or chill it to bake or broil later.

3 cups water
1 cup cornmeal
1 cup cold water
½ teaspoon salt
¾ cup freshly grated Asiago or Parmesan cheese
    Nonstick spray coating
1 15-ounce can chunky tomato sauce with onion, celery, and green sweet pepper
1¼ cups skim milk
2 tablespoons all-purpose flour
1 tablespoon snipped fresh basil or ½ teaspoon dried basil, crushed
¼ teaspoon salt
⅛ teaspoon pepper
    Dash ground nutmeg

● For polenta, in a medium saucepan bring the 3 cups water to boiling. In a small bowl combine the cornmeal, water, and salt. Slowly add the cornmeal mixture to the boiling water, stirring constantly. Cook and stir until mixture returns to boiling. Reduce heat to low. Cook, uncovered, for 10 to 15 minutes or until thick, stirring frequently. Stir in ¼ *cup* of the Asiago or Parmesan cheese, stirring until melted.

● Spray an 8×8-inch baking pan with nonstick coating. Spread hot polenta evenly into the pan; cool slightly. Cover; chill 2 hours or overnight. Cut polenta into 1-inch squares; set aside.

● Meanwhile, for sauces, in a medium saucepan bring tomato sauce to boiling; reduce heat. Simmer, uncovered, about 10 minutes or until slightly thickened.

● For white sauce, in a medium saucepan gradually stir the milk into the flour, basil, salt, pepper, and nutmeg. Cook and stir over medium heat until thickened and bubbly. Cook and stir for 1 minute more. Remove from heat; stir in another ¼ *cup* of cheese, stirring until melted.

● To assemble, divide red sauce among individual shallow casseroles (a scant ¼ cup each). Divide polenta cubes among casseroles. Spoon white sauce over cubes; sprinkle each serving with 1 tablespoon of the remaining ¼ cup cheese. Bake in a 450° oven for 12 to 15 minutes or until sauce is bubbly and the cheese begins to brown. Serve immediately. Makes 4 servings.

TOTAL FAT: 7 g
DAILY VALUE FAT: 10%
SATURATED FAT: 4 g
DAILY VALUE SATURATED FAT: 20%

NUTRITION FACTS
PER SERVING:

Calories	278
Total Fat	7 g
Saturated Fat	4 g
Cholesterol	20 mg
Sodium	733 mg
Carbohydrate	41 g
Fiber	4 g
Protein	13 g

EXCHANGES:
2½ Starch
1 Vegetable
½ Lean Meat
1 Fat

PREPARATION TIME: 20 minutes
CHILLING TIME: 2 hours
BAKING TIME: 12 minutes

TOTAL FAT: 3 g
DAILY VALUE FAT: 4%
SATURATED FAT: 2 g
DAILY VALUE SATURATED FAT: 10%

NUTRITION FACTS
PER SERVING:

Calories	297
Total Fat	3 g
Saturated Fat	2 g
Cholesterol	14 mg
Sodium	626 mg
Carbohydrate	51 g
Fiber	3 g
Protein	17 g

EXCHANGES:
3 Starch
½ Medium-Fat Meat
½ Milk

PREPARATION TIME: 1 hour and 40 minutes
COOKING TIME: 20 minutes

Potato Gnocchi in
Basil Cream Sauce

Peeling the potatoes after they're cooked keeps them from absorbing too much liquid during cooking, which can make your gnocchi (NYOH-kee) too wet.

1 **pound baking potatoes (such as Russet or round white potatoes)**
2 **tablespoons snipped fresh chives or parsley**
½ **teaspoon salt**
¼ **teaspoon pepper**
¾ **to 1 cup all-purpose flour**
2 **tablespoons all-purpose flour**
⅛ **teaspoon garlic powder**
1 **12-ounce can evaporated skim milk**
2 **tablespoons snipped fresh basil**
2 **ounces prosciutto or cooked ham, chopped (½ cup)**
¼ **cup shredded Parmesan cheese**
   Snipped fresh basil

● For potatoes, prick skins with a fork. Bake in a 425° oven for 40 to 60 minutes or until tender. (Or, cook whole, unpeeled potatoes in boiling water for 20 to 25 minutes or until tender. Drain.) When cool enough to handle, peel and cut up potatoes. Mash potatoes with a potato masher or run through a food mill or ricer.

● In a medium bowl combine potatoes, chives or parsley, salt, and pepper. Stir with a fork until combined. Using a wooden spoon, stir in enough of the ¾ to 1 cup flour to form dough into a ball.

● On a lightly floured surface, knead in enough remaining flour to make a dough that is firm and not sticky (this will take about 3 minutes). Divide dough into 4 portions; divide each into 16 portions (64 total). Form dough into balls.

● Place 1 ball at a time onto a floured fork; press with finger to flatten slightly. (Gnocchi should have ridges on one side and a depression on the other.) Transfer to a baking sheet lined with waxed paper. (If desired, cover and chill gnocchi until ready to cook or for up to 12 hours.)

● In a 3-quart saucepan cook the gnocchi, *half* at a time, in a large amount of gently boiling, lightly salted *water* for 1 to 2 minutes or until gnocchi rise to the top and have a breadlike texture. Remove gnocchi with a slotted spoon. Keep warm.

● For sauce, in a saucepan stir together the 2 tablespoons flour and the garlic powder. Gradually whisk in milk. Cook and stir over medium heat until bubbly. Cook and stir for 1 minute more. Stir in the 2 tablespoons basil and the prosciutto or ham. Heat through. To serve, stir together gnocchi and sauce. Sprinkle with cheese and additional basil. Serves 4.

Baked Gnocchi
With Tomato-Basil Sauce

Gnocchi can also be made from semolina flour or farina, rather than potatoes as on the preceding page. All you need to complete the meal for this basil-infused dish is a salad.

3 cups skim milk
¾ cup semolina or quick-cooking farina
¼ teaspoon salt
   Dash ground nutmeg
2 beaten eggs
½ cup finely shredded Parmesan cheese
   Nonstick spray coating
1 tablespoon olive oil
1 recipe Tomato-Basil Sauce or spaghetti sauce

● In a medium saucepan heat *2 cups* of the milk until boiling. Combine remaining milk, semolina or farina, salt, and nutmeg; pour into boiling milk mixture, stirring constantly. Cook and stir about 5 minutes or until very thick. Remove from heat. Stir about *1 cup* of the hot mixture into the eggs; return to mixture in pan. Cook and stir 2 minutes more; remove from heat. Stir in *half* of the cheese. Line a 13×9×2-inch baking pan with foil so foil extends over edges; spray with nonstick coating. Pour mixture into pan, spreading evenly. Cover and chill for at least 30 minutes or until firm.

● Using foil, lift semolina mixture from pan to a cutting board. With 2-inch round cutter, cut semolina mixture into circles. Overlap circles in a greased 13×9×2-inch baking pan. Place the remaining pieces around edges. Brush lightly with oil; sprinkle with the remaining cheese. Bake in a 425° oven for 25 to 30 minutes or until golden brown. (Prepare sauce while baking gnocchi; keep gnocchi warm after baking.) Serve with Tomato-Basil Sauce or spaghetti sauce. Makes 6 servings.

Tomato-Basil Sauce: In a medium saucepan cook ½ cup finely chopped *onion* and 2 cloves *garlic,* minced, in small amount of *water* until onion is tender. Drain off water. Stir in 4 cups peeled, seeded, and chopped ripe *tomatoes* (3 pounds),* ¼ teaspoon *salt,* and ⅛ teaspoon *pepper.* Bring to boiling; reduce heat. Boil gently, uncovered, for 35 minutes, or until slightly thickened. Stir in ¼ cup snipped *fresh basil* or 1½ teaspoons *dried basil,* crushed. Cook about 5 minutes more or until of desired consistency. Serve over gnocchi or hot cooked pasta. Makes 2½ cups.

*Note: Two 14½-ounce cans of whole Italian-style tomatoes, undrained and cut up, can be substituted for the fresh tomatoes. Decrease the salt to ⅛ teaspoon and cook the mixture only 18 to 20 minutes before adding basil.

TOTAL FAT: 7 g
DAILY VALUE FAT: 10%
SATURATED FAT: 1 g
DAILY VALUE SATURATED FAT: 5%

**NUTRITION FACTS
PER SERVING:**

Calories	237
Total Fat	7 g
Saturated Fat	1 g
Cholesterol	80 mg
Sodium	382 mg
Carbohydrate	30 g
Fiber	2 g
Protein	14 g

EXCHANGES:
1½ Starch
1 Vegetable
1 Lean Meat
½ Fat

PREPARATION TIME: 15 minutes
CHILLING TIME: 30 minutes
BAKING TIME: 25 minutes

**NUTRITION FACTS
PER SERVING:**

Calories	249
Total Fat	9 g
Saturated Fat	3 g
Cholesterol	18 mg
Sodium	292 mg
Carbohydrate	28 g
Fiber	3 g
Protein	17 g

EXCHANGES:
1 Starch
2 Vegetable
1½ Medium-Fat Meat

**PREPARATION TIME: 55 minutes
BAKING TIME: 35 minutes
STANDING TIME: 10 minutes**

Vegetable Lasagna
With Red Pepper Sauce

In a hurry? Substitute 2 cups of prepared spaghetti sauce for the Red Pepper Sauce in this recipe.

6 no-boil lasagna noodles or regular lasagna noodles
8 ounces zucchini and/or yellow summer squash, halved and sliced
2 cups sliced fresh mushrooms
⅓ cup chopped onion
2 teaspoons olive oil
1 cup fat-free or low-fat ricotta cheese
¼ cup finely shredded Parmesan cheese
¼ teaspoon black pepper
1 recipe Red Pepper Sauce
1 cup shredded part-skim mozzarella cheese
1 medium tomato, seeded and chopped

● Soak the no-boil lasagna noodles in warm water for 10 minutes. (Or, cook regular noodles according to package directions, *except* omit salt.)

● Meanwhile, in a large skillet cook and stir zucchini or yellow summer squash, mushrooms, and onion in hot oil over medium heat for 6 minutes or until zucchini is tender. Drain well.

● In a small bowl stir together ricotta cheese, Parmesan cheese, and black pepper. To assemble, place 3 lasagna noodles in a 2-quart square baking dish, trimming to fit as necessary. Top with ricotta mixture, *half* of the vegetable mixture, *half* of the Red Pepper Sauce, and *half* of the mozzarella cheese. Layer with remaining lasagna noodles, vegetables, and sauce.

● Bake lasagna, uncovered, in a 375° oven for 30 minutes. Sprinkle with remaining mozzarella cheese and the tomato; bake 5 minutes more or until heated through. Let stand 10 minutes before serving. Makes 6 servings.

Red Pepper Sauce: In a large skillet cook 3 cups chopped *red sweet peppers* and 4 whole cloves *garlic* in 1 tablespoon *olive oil* over medium heat about 20 minutes, stirring occasionally. (Or, you may use one 12-ounce jar roasted red sweet peppers, drained. Omit cooking step.) Place pepper mixture in a blender container. Cover; blend until nearly smooth. Add ½ cup *water,* ¼ cup *tomato paste,* 2 tablespoons *red wine vinegar,* and 1 tablespoon snipped *fresh oregano* or ½ teaspoon *dried oregano,* crushed. Cover; blend with several on-off turns until oregano is just chopped and mixture is nearly smooth. Return to skillet. Cook and stir over medium heat until heated through. Makes about 2 cups.

TOTAL FAT: 8 g
DAILY VALUE FAT: 12%
SATURATED FAT: 1 g
DAILY VALUE SATURATED FAT: 5%

NUTRITION FACTS
PER SERVING:

Calories	365
Total Fat	8 g
Saturated Fat	1 g
Cholesterol	54 mg
Sodium	809 mg
Carbohydrate	59 g
Fiber	4 g
Protein	17 g

EXCHANGES:
3 Starch
3 Vegetable
1 Medium-Fat Meat
½ Fat

PREPARATION TIME: 25 minutes
COOKING TIME: 30 minutes

Chunky Tomato Sauce
With Tortellini

This quick-to-prepare tomato sauce also makes a tasty topping for spaghetti. Make a double batch and freeze half in an airtight container for later.

1 cup chopped onion
½ cup coarsely chopped green sweet pepper
¼ cup coarsely chopped carrot
2 cloves garlic, minced
2 teaspoons olive oil
3 large tomatoes, peeled and chopped
   (2 cups), or one 14½-ounce can
   tomatoes, cut up
½ of 6-ounce can (⅓ cup) tomato paste
¼ cup water
¾ teaspoon dried basil, crushed
½ teaspoon sugar
¼ teaspoon salt
¼ teaspoon dried thyme, crushed
1 9-ounce package refrigerated
   cheese-filled tortellini or
   mushroom-filled tortellini

● In a large skillet cook onion, sweet pepper, carrot, and garlic in hot oil about 5 minutes or until vegetables are tender.

● Carefully stir in the fresh or *undrained* canned tomatoes, tomato paste, water, basil, sugar, salt, and thyme. Bring to boiling; reduce heat. Cover and simmer for 30 minutes, stirring occasionally. If necessary, uncover and simmer for 5 to 10 minutes more or until of desired consistency, stirring constantly.

● Meanwhile, cook pasta according to package directions. Drain. Immediately serve with sauce. Makes 3 servings.

Spinach and Pasta Rolls

These pretty pasta rolls are perfect for entertaining. Make them ahead and pop them in the oven when your guests arrive.

3   sheets (10×7 inches each) ready-to-use
    frozen lasagna sheets*
2¼   cups skim milk
2   tablespoons cornstarch
⅛   teaspoon ground nutmeg
1   tablespoon finely snipped fresh basil
½   cup finely shredded Parmesan cheese
1   10-ounce package frozen chopped
    spinach
1   beaten egg
1¼   cups fat-free ricotta cheese
3   ounces reduced-fat cream cheese
    (Neufchâtel), softened
2   tablespoons thinly sliced green onion
    Nonstick spray coating
    Shredded fresh basil leaves (optional)
    Chopped tomatoes (optional)

● Place frozen lasagna sheets on a baking sheet; cover with plastic wrap and let stand to thaw for 30 minutes. Drain. Set aside.

● For sauce, in a small saucepan combine milk, cornstarch, and nutmeg. Cook and stir over medium heat until bubbly. Cook and stir for 1 minute more. Remove from heat. Stir in the 1 tablespoon snipped basil and the Parmesan cheese. Reserve ⅓ *cup* of the sauce.

● For filling, cook spinach according to package directions. Drain well, pressing out excess liquid with the back of a spoon. In a medium mixing bowl stir together the egg, ricotta cheese, cream cheese, and green onion. Add the spinach and reserved sauce; mix well. Set aside.

● To assemble, place a thawed lasagna sheet on a work surface. Spoon about *one-third* of the cheese mixture over the sheet. Starting from the short edge, roll up, jelly-roll style. Cut crosswise into 6 pieces. Spray a 2-quart rectangular baking dish with nonstick coating. Place pasta rolls, seam sides down, in dish. Repeat with remaining lasagna sheets. Pour remaining sauce over rolls.

● Cover and refrigerate pasta rolls for up to 24 hours. (Or, bake immediately, uncovered, in a 350° oven for 35 to 40 minutes or until heated through.) To serve, bake the chilled casserole, covered, in a 350° oven for 50 to 55 minutes or until heated through. If desired, top with basil and tomatoes. Makes 6 servings.

Note: Or, use 12 regular lasagna noodles; cook according to package directions. Place a halved noodle on a work surface. Spoon a scant ¼ cup of cheese mixture onto the noodle. Roll up, jelly-roll style. Repeat with remaining noodles.

TOTAL FAT: 7 g
DAILY VALUE FAT: 10%
SATURATED FAT: 4 g
DAILY VALUE SATURATED FAT: 20%

NUTRITION FACTS
PER SERVING:

Calories	211
Total Fat	7 g
Saturated Fat	4 g
Cholesterol	62 mg
Sodium	324 mg
Carbohydrate	20 g
Fiber	1 g
Protein	18 g

EXCHANGES:
1 Starch
2 Lean Meat
¼ Milk

PREPARATION TIME: 45 minutes
COOKING TIME: 35 minutes

TOTAL FAT: 2 g
DAILY VALUE FAT: 3%
SATURATED FAT: 1 g
DAILY VALUE SATURATED FAT: 5%

NUTRITION FACTS
PER SERVING:

Calories	146
Total Fat	2 g
Saturated Fat	1 g
Cholesterol	53 mg
Sodium	150 mg
Carbohydrate	26 g
Fiber	1 g
Protein	5 g

EXCHANGES:
1½ Starch
½ Fat

PREPARATION TIME: 40 minutes
RESTING TIME: 30 minutes total

Homemade Pasta

Making pasta is actually easier than you might think, and the flavor possibilities are endless.

2½ **cups all-purpose flour**
½ **teaspoon salt**
2 **beaten eggs**
⅓ **cup water**
1 **teaspoon olive oil or cooking oil**

● In a large mixing bowl stir together *2 cups* of the flour and the salt. Make a well in the center of the mixture. In a small bowl stir together eggs, water, and oil. Add to flour mixture; mix well.

● Sprinkle kneading surface with the remaining flour. Turn dough out onto floured surface. Knead until dough is smooth and elastic (8 to 10 minutes total). Cover; let rest for 10 minutes.

● Divide dough into fourths. On a lightly floured surface, roll each fourth into a 12-inch square (about ⅟₁₆ inch thick). Let dough stand about 20 minutes or until slightly dry. Shape as desired (see box, below). (Or, if using a pasta machine, pass each fourth of dough through the machine according to manufacturer's directions, until ⅟₁₆ inch thick. Shape as directed.)

● Cook pasta, allowing a few more minutes for dried or frozen pasta. Drain well. Makes 1 pound pasta (8 servings).

Herb Pasta: Prepare pasta as directed, *except* add 1 teaspoon crushed *dried basil, marjoram,* or *sage* to the flour mixture.
Spinach Pasta: Prepare pasta as directed, *except* reduce the water to 3 tablespoons and add ⅓ cup very finely chopped, well-drained, cooked *spinach* to the egg mixture.

Shaping and Storing Pasta

Lasagna: Cut the dough into strips about 2½ inches wide. Cut into desired lengths.
Farfalle: Cut into 2×1-inch rectangles. Pinch centers to form a bow tie.
Tripolini: Cut into 1-inch circles. Pinch centers, forming butterfly shapes.
Linguine or fettuccine: After rolling dough and letting it stand, loosely roll up dough, jelly-roll style; cut into ⅛-inch-wide slices for linguine or ¼-inch-wide slices for fettuccine. Shake strands to separate. Cut into desired lengths.

To store pasta: After cutting and shaping pasta, spread it on a wire rack or hang it from a pasta drying rack or clothes hanger. Let dry overnight or until completely dry. Place pasta in an airtight container and refrigerate for up to 3 days. Or, dry pasta at least 1 hour. Seal in a moisture- and vapor-proof plastic bag or container. Freeze for up to 8 months.

Pasta Primavera

Primavera in Italian means "spring style," and fresh vegetables make this dish springlike. Use your favorites to vary the recipe. Asparagus (in place of the beans) makes an excellent choice.

5 ounces corkscrew macaroni or fettuccine
8 ounces fresh wax or green beans, cut into 2-inch pieces (2 cups), or one 9-ounce package frozen French-style green beans
¼ cup water
2 cups sliced fresh mushrooms
¼ cup coarsely chopped green or red sweet pepper
1 clove garlic, minced
¼ teaspoon salt
¼ teaspoon black pepper
1 12-ounce can evaporated skim milk
4 teaspoons cornstarch
½ cup shredded provolone or mozzarella cheese (2 ounces)
Pine nuts (optional)

● Cook pasta according to package directions, *except* cook *fresh* green beans (if using) with the pasta; drain well.

● Meanwhile, in a saucepan combine water, mushrooms, frozen green beans (if using), sweet pepper, garlic, salt, and pepper. Bring to boiling; reduce heat. Cover; simmer for 4 minutes or until vegetables are tender. *Do not drain.*

● Stir together the milk and cornstarch; stir into vegetable mixture. Cook and stir over medium heat until thickened and bubbly. Cook and stir for 1 minute more. Stir in cheese until melted. To serve, pour sauce over pasta and bean mixture. If desired, garnish with pine nuts. Makes 4 servings.

Best-Bet Vegetables

It's hard to beat the flavor of fresh vegetables when cooked to perfection, but fresh vegetables may not always be your best buy. Unless homegrown or grown locally, produce may not reach your market for several days. During that long trip, vegetables may lose flavor, moisture, and nutrients. Commercially harvested produce usually is frozen or canned within 4 to 6 hours of harvesting, when nutrient content is high. Some nutrients are lost during processing, but the shorter the time between harvesting and processing, the better the nutrients are retained. When deciding between fresh, canned, and frozen vegetables, choose what best meets the needs and tastes of your family.

TOTAL FAT: 5 g
DAILY VALUE FAT: 7%
SATURATED FAT: 3 g
DAILY VALUE SATURATED FAT: 15%

NUTRITION FACTS
PER SERVING:

Calories	296
Total Fat	5 g
Saturated Fat	3 g
Cholesterol	13 mg
Sodium	360 mg
Carbohydrate	47 g
Fiber	2 g
Protein	17 g

EXCHANGES:
2 Starch
1 Vegetable
½ Medium-Fat Meat
1 Milk
½ Fat

PREPARATION TIME: 15 minutes
COOKING TIME: 10 minutes

TOTAL FAT: 8 g
DAILY VALUE FAT: 12%
SATURATED FAT: 3 g
DAILY VALUE SATURATED FAT: 15%

NUTRITION FACTS
PER SERVING:

Calories	415
Total Fat	8 g
Saturated Fat	3 g
Cholesterol	19 mg
Sodium	654 mg
Carbohydrate	68 g
Fiber	6 g
Protein	22 g

EXCHANGES:
3 Starch
2½ Vegetable
1 Lean Meat
½ Milk
½ Fat

ROASTING TIME: 35 minutes for garlic
PREPARATION TIME: 25 minutes
COOKING TIME: 35 minutes

Fettuccine
With Roasted Garlic Sauce

Roast extra garlic bulbs for a mellow paste and try it as a delicious, fat-free spread for crusty Italian bread.

2 large garlic bulbs
1 8- or 9-ounce package frozen artichoke hearts
¾ cup chopped red sweet pepper
12 ounces refrigerated spinach fettuccine
1 12-ounce can evaporated skim milk
2 teaspoons all-purpose flour
¼ teaspoon salt
¼ teaspoon lemon-pepper seasoning
2 ounces reduced-fat cream cheese (Neufchâtel)
¼ cup freshly grated Parmesan cheese

● For garlic paste, cut ½ inch off the pointed top portions of garlic bulbs. Remove the outer papery layers of the garlic. Place both bulbs of garlic on a square piece of foil. Bring edges of foil together to form a pouch. Seal. Bake garlic in a 375° oven for 25 to 35 minutes or until very soft. When cool enough to handle, use your fingers to press garlic pulp from each clove. Mash pulp with a spoon or fork to make a smooth paste (you should have about 2 tablespoons). Set paste aside.

● Cut up any large pieces of artichoke hearts. Cook artichoke hearts according to package directions, *except* add sweet pepper during last minute of cooking; drain. Return to saucepan.

● Meanwhile, cook pasta according to package directions. Drain. Cover to keep warm.

● In a screw-top jar combine milk, flour, salt, and lemon-pepper seasoning; cover and shake until smooth. Add the garlic paste. Stir garlic mixture into artichoke mixture in saucepan. Cook and stir over medium heat until mixture is thickened and bubbly. Cook and stir 1 minute more. Stir in cream cheese until melted. Heat through. Serve over hot pasta. Sprinkle with Parmesan cheese. Makes 4 servings.

129
Main Dishes

Orzo-Stuffed Peppers

Orzo is a rice-shaped dried pasta that can be added to soups and stews, or cooked and served as a side dish. In the stuffing for these peppers, orzo stands in for the traditional rice.

2 large yellow, red, or green sweet peppers, halved lengthwise
⅔ cup packaged dried orzo (rosamarina)
1 clove garlic, minced
1 tablespoon olive oil or cooking oil
4 teaspoons all-purpose flour
¼ teaspoon salt
⅛ teaspoon black pepper
¾ cup skim milk
1 large tomato, peeled, seeded, and chopped (¾ cup)
¼ cup thinly sliced green onion
⅓ cup shredded provolone cheese (1½ ounces)
1 tablespoon snipped fresh mint or 2 tablespoons snipped fresh basil, or ½ teaspoon dried mint or 1 teaspoon dried basil, crushed
2 tablespoons grated Asiago or Parmesan cheese

● Remove stems, membranes, and seeds from sweet peppers. In a covered saucepan cook peppers in a large amount of boiling *water* for 3 minutes. Drain well. Cook orzo according to package directions; drain and set aside.

● For filling, in a small saucepan cook the garlic in hot oil for 1 minute. Stir in the flour, salt, and black pepper. Add the milk all at once. Cook and stir until thickened and bubbly. Stir in the cooked orzo, tomato, green onion, provolone cheese, and mint or basil.

● Place the sweet pepper halves in a 2-quart square baking dish. Spoon filling into peppers and spoon any remaining filling around peppers. Sprinkle with Asiago or Parmesan cheese. Bake in a 375° oven for 20 to 25 minutes or until heated through. Makes 4 servings.

TOTAL FAT: 8 g
DAILY VALUE FAT: 12%
SATURATED FAT: 3 g
DAILY VALUE SATURATED FAT: 15%

NUTRITION FACTS
PER SERVING:

Calories	198
Total Fat	8 g
Saturated Fat	3 g
Cholesterol	11 mg
Sodium	265 mg
Carbohydrate	24 g
Fiber	3 g
Protein	9 g

EXCHANGES:
1 Starch
1 Vegetable
½ High-Fat Meat
1 Fat

PREPARATION TIME: 25 minutes
COOKING TIME: 20 minutes

Baked Potatoes and Mushrooms, recipe on page 132

Artichokes Parmesan,
recipe on page 133

Side Dishes

Choosing an entrée to make for dinner is usually easy. Sometimes the more difficult thing is coming up with an accompaniment. These side dishes make it simple, whether it's an all-out Italian bash you're planning or just an everyday dinner. Few can resist a casserole full of oven-browned Baked Potatoes and Mushrooms (page 132) or caramelized Sweet-and-Sour Onions (page 135) that are splashed with a little balsamic vinegar. Country-Style Peas (page 141), Zucchini alla Romana (page 138), and Grilled Stuffed Eggplant (page 136) also make any meal more special.

TOTAL FAT: 5 g
DAILY VALUE FAT: 7%
SATURATED FAT: 2 g
DAILY VALUE SATURATED FAT: 10%

NUTRITION FACTS
PER SERVING:

Calories	167
Total Fat	5 g
Saturated Fat	2 g
Cholesterol	8 mg
Sodium	297 mg
Carbohydrate	22 g
Fiber	2 g
Protein	8 g

EXCHANGES:
1½ Starch
½ Lean Meat
½ Fat

PREPARATION TIME: 45 minutes
BAKING TIME: 1 hour and 10 minutes
STANDING TIME: 5 minutes

Baked Potatoes
And Mushrooms

The dried mushrooms in this dish add a rich, earthy flavor. After soaking and draining the mushrooms, rinse them well to remove all traces of grit. (Pictured on page 130.)

½ cup dried porcini or morel mushrooms (about ⅜ ounce)
1 small onion, thinly sliced
1 tablespoon olive oil or margarine
2 tablespoons all-purpose flour
¼ teaspoon salt
⅛ teaspoon pepper
1¼ cups skim milk
½ cup freshly shredded pecorino cheese or Parmesan cheese (2 ounces)
3 medium baking potatoes, peeled and thinly sliced (3 cups)

● In a small bowl place mushrooms in enough *warm water* to cover. Let soak for 30 minutes. Drain. Coarsely chop.

● For sauce, cook mushrooms and onion in hot oil or margarine until onion is tender. Stir in flour, salt, and pepper. Add milk all at once. Cook and stir until thickened and bubbly. Remove from heat. Stir *half* of the cheese into the sauce. Place *half* of the sliced potatoes in a greased 1-quart casserole. Cover with *half* of the sauce. Repeat layering. Sprinkle with the remaining cheese.

● Bake, covered, in a 350° oven for 35 minutes. Uncover; bake 35 minutes more or until potatoes are tender and top is golden brown. Let stand 5 minutes before serving. Makes 6 servings.

Potato Pointers

If you avoid potatoes because you think they're fattening, there's no need. It's really what you top them with that matters. Overdoing the margarine or butter and cheese is what causes the calories to climb. Here we've used just a little olive oil and cheese to add flavor without the guilt. Remember to always use full-flavored cheeses, such as aged fresh Parmesan and sharp cheddar, and oils, such as olive or sesame, which pack lots of flavor in small amounts.

Artichokes Parmesan

Eating artichokes is an art. Use your fingers to pull off the leaves, one at a time, and draw each leaf through your teeth, scraping off the tender meat inside the base of the leaf. Discard the rest of the tough leaf. Eat the meaty bottom portion of the artichoke with a fork. (Pictured on pages 130 and 131.)

3 medium artichokes
Lemon juice
2 cups soft bread crumbs
1½ cups peeled, seeded, and chopped tomato
¼ cup grated Parmesan or Romano cheese
1 tablespoon snipped parsley
1 tablespoon snipped fresh mint or fresh basil
1 clove garlic, minced

● Remove stems and loosen outer leaves from artichokes. Cut off 1 inch from tops of leaves; cut in half lengthwise. Brush edges with the lemon juice.

● In large covered kettle cook artichokes in boiling salted *water* for 20 to 30 minutes or until a leaf pulls out easily. Drain cut side down. Remove center leaves and the fuzzy "choke." Sprinkle insides lightly with *salt*.

● Combine bread crumbs, tomato, Parmesan or Romano cheese, parsley, mint or basil, and garlic. Spoon mixture into artichokes. Place in a 13×9×2-inch baking pan. Cover and bake in a 375° oven for 15 minutes. Uncover; bake about 10 to 15 minutes more or until tops are lightly golden brown. Makes 6 servings.

TOTAL FAT: 2 g
DAILY VALUE FAT: 3%
SATURATED FAT: 1 g
DAILY VALUE SATURATED FAT: 5%

NUTRITION FACTS PER SERVING:

Calories	99
Total Fat	2 g
Saturated Fat	1 g
Cholesterol	3 mg
Sodium	216 mg
Carbohydrate	16 g
Fiber	3 g
Protein	5 g

EXCHANGES:
½ Starch
1½ Vegetable
½ Fat

PREPARATION TIME: 45 minutes
BAKING TIME: 25 minutes

Sweet-and-Sour Onions

These onions in a piquant sauce of vinegar and brown sugar make a perfect accompaniment to roasted beef, pork, or chicken.

3 cups pearl white and/or red onions, or one 16-ounce package frozen small whole onions
2 teaspoons margarine
¼ cup white wine vinegar or balsamic vinegar
2 tablespoons brown sugar
⅛ teaspoon pepper
1 ounce prosciutto or thinly sliced cooked ham, cut into short thin strips

● In a medium saucepan bring about ½ cup *water* to boiling; add unpeeled pearl onions. Return to boiling; reduce heat. Cover and cook about 10 minutes or until just tender. Drain onions. Cool slightly; trim ends and remove skin. (Or, cook frozen onions in a medium saucepan according to package directions and drain.)

● In the same saucepan melt the margarine over medium heat; stir in vinegar, brown sugar, and pepper. Cook and stir about 30 seconds or until combined. Add onions and prosciutto or ham to saucepan. Cook, uncovered, over medium heat for 7 to 8 minutes more or until onions are golden brown and slightly glazed, stirring occasionally. Makes 4 servings.

Vitalizing Veggies

Everyone knows vegetables are good for you, but do you know why? Vegetables provide our bodies with vitamins A and C, folic acid, iron, magnesium, and other important nutrients. In addition, they're low in fat and high in fiber. Vegetables are so important to our diets, that health experts recommend 3 to 5 servings a day. But can we really eat that much? You bet. It's easy to meet your minimum goal for the day, or even exceed it, when you consider that the following equals a serving:

● 1 cup of raw leafy vegetables, such as spinach, cabbage, or lettuce
● ½ cup of chopped vegetables, such as carrots, potatoes, or corn, cooked or raw
● ¾ cup vegetable juice

TOTAL FAT: 2 g
DAILY VALUE FAT: 3%
SATURATED FAT: 0 g
DAILY VALUE SATURATED FAT: 0%

NUTRITION FACTS PER SERVING:

Calories	94
Total Fat	2 g
Saturated Fat	0 g
Cholesterol	3 mg
Sodium	372 mg
Carbohydrate	16 g
Fiber	2 g
Protein	3 g

EXCHANGES:
½ Fruit
1½ Vegetable
½ Fat

START TO FINISH: 35 minutes

TOTAL FAT: 5 g
DAILY VALUE FAT: 7%
SATURATED FAT: 1 g
DAILY VALUE SATURATED FAT: 5%

NUTRITION FACTS
PER SERVING:

Calories	90
Total Fat	5 g
Saturated Fat	1 g
Cholesterol	2 mg
Sodium	331 mg
Carbohydrate	11 g
Fiber	4 g
Protein	3 g

EXCHANGES:
2 Vegetable
1 Fat

PREPARATION TIME: 15 minutes
GRILLING TIME: 20 minutes

Grilled Stuffed Eggplant

Grilling the eggplant in foil packets makes cleanup a snap.

1　medium eggplant (1 pound)
1　cup sliced fresh mushrooms
½　cup chopped green sweet pepper
⅓　cup finely chopped onion
1　clove garlic, minced
½　teaspoon dried basil, crushed
1　tablespoon olive oil or cooking oil
1　medium tomato, chopped
½　teaspoon salt
2　tablespoons finely shredded or grated
　　Parmesan cheese

● Preheat coals in a covered grill while preparing eggplant. Arrange preheated coals around a drip pan in a covered grill. Test for *medium* heat above pan.

● Meanwhile, cut eggplant in half lengthwise. Using a grapefruit knife, hollow out eggplant, leaving a ¼-inch-thick shell. Chop eggplant pulp (you should have about 2½ cups).

● In a large skillet cook chopped eggplant, mushrooms, sweet pepper, onion, garlic, and basil in hot oil over medium heat until nearly tender, stirring occasionally. Stir in tomato and salt. Spoon mixture into eggplant shells. Sprinkle with Parmesan cheese.

● Tear two 24×18-inch pieces of heavy foil. Fold each piece in half to make two double thicknesses of foil that measure 18×12 inches. Place an eggplant half on each. For each packet, bring up two opposite edges of the foil piece and seal with a double fold. Fold remaining ends of each piece to completely enclose eggplant halves, leaving space for steam to build inside.

● Place eggplant packets on grill over drip pan. Cover and grill for 20 to 25 minutes or until eggplant shells are tender. (Or, to bake, place the foil packets on a 15×10×1-inch baking pan. Bake the stuffed eggplants in a 375° oven for 25 to 30 minutes or until tender.) Makes 4 servings.

Broiled Eggplant with Cheese

This quick eggplant dish is easy on the waistline, too, with only 92 calories and 5 grams of fat per serving.

1 **medium eggplant (1 pound)**
2 **tablespoons finely chopped green onion**
1 **tablespoon olive oil or cooking oil**
1 **tablespoon balsamic vinegar**
2 **cloves garlic, minced**
 Dash crushed red pepper
⅓ **cup shredded reduced-fat mozzarella cheese (1½ ounces)**
1 **teaspoon dried oregano, crushed, or 1 tablespoon snipped fresh oregano**
 Fresh oregano (optional)

● Wash eggplant; cut crosswise into 16 slices, about ½ inch thick. Place eggplant slices on the unheated rack of a broiler pan. Broil 4 to 5 inches from heat for 4 to 5 minutes.

● Meanwhile, combine the green onion, oil, vinegar, garlic, and crushed red pepper. Turn eggplant over and brush with onion mixture. Broil 4 to 5 minutes more or until eggplant is tender.

● Sprinkle cheese and dried oregano (if using) over eggplant slices. Broil for 1 minute more. Sprinkle with 1 tablespoon fresh oregano (if using). If desired, garnish with fresh oregano. Serve immediately. Makes 4 servings.

Where's the Hen?

Despite its name, the dark purple pear-shaped eggplant doesn't come from a hen. But this long slender fruit is popular in Italy. There are several types of eggplants available, such as western, white, Japanese, and small (baby) eggplants. When selecting eggplants, look for plump, glossy, heavy fruits. Don't buy the ones that have scarring, bruising, or dull skins. The green stem cap should be fresh, unshriveled, and free of mold. Refrigerate them after purchasing, for up to 2 days.

TOTAL FAT: 5 g
DAILY VALUE FAT: 7%
SATURATED FAT: 2 g
DAILY VALUE SATURATED FAT: 10%

NUTRITION FACTS PER SERVING:

Calories	92
Total Fat	5 g
Saturated Fat	2 g
Cholesterol	5 mg
Sodium	53 mg
Carbohydrate	9 g
Fiber	3 g
Protein	4 g

EXCHANGES:
2 Vegetable
1 Fat

PREPARATION TIME: 10 minutes
COOKING TIME: 8 minutes

TOTAL FAT: 2 g
DAILY VALUE FAT: 3%
SATURATED FAT: 1 g
DAILY VALUE SATURATED FAT: 5%

NUTRITION FACTS
PER SERVING:

Calories	35
Total Fat	2 g
Saturated Fat	1 g
Cholesterol	2 mg
Sodium	130 mg
Carbohydrate	3 g
Fiber	1 g
Protein	2 g

EXCHANGES:
1 Vegetable
½ Fat

PREPARATION TIME: 8 minutes
COOKING TIME: 5 minutes

Zucchini alla Romana

For best results, select zucchini that are small, firm, and free of cuts and soft spots. Pass over large zucchini. They tend to have tough skins and lots of seeds. If you're lucky enough to find baby squash, use them instead.

2 cloves garlic
2 teaspoons olive oil
4 cups sliced zucchini
1 teaspoon dried mint or dried basil, crushed, or 1 tablespoon snipped fresh mint or fresh basil
¼ teaspoon salt
   Dash pepper
2 tablespoons finely shredded Parmesan or Romano cheese

● In a large skillet cook whole garlic cloves in hot oil until lightly brown; discard garlic. Add zucchini, dried mint or basil (if using), salt, and pepper to oil in skillet. Cook, uncovered, over medium heat about 5 minutes or until zucchini is crisp-tender, stirring occasionally. To serve, sprinkle with Parmesan cheese and fresh mint or basil (if using). Makes 6 servings.

Keeping Fresh Herbs Fresh

When buying herbs by the bunch, store them in a loose-fitting bag in the crisper drawer of your refrigerator. Perennial herbs (sage, marjoram, oregano, thyme, rosemary, and tarragon) will last for weeks. Annual herbs (basil, chervil, cilantro, dill, and parsley) are more fragile; use them within a few days.

TOTAL FAT: 5 g
DAILY VALUE FAT: 7%
SATURATED FAT: 1 g
DAILY VALUE SATURATED FAT: 5%

NUTRITION FACTS
PER SERVING:

Calories	94
Total Fat	5 g
Saturated Fat	1 g
Cholesterol	1 mg
Sodium	220 mg
Carbohydrate	11 g
Fiber	2 g
Protein	3 g

EXCHANGES:
2 Vegetable
1 Fat

PREPARATION TIME: 8 minutes
COOKING TIME: 3 minutes

Roma-Style Spinach

If you don't have any fresh spinach on hand, you can substitute one 10-ounce package of frozen chopped spinach, cooked and well-drained. Just add it to the cooked raisin mixture and serve.

¼ cup golden raisins
2 tablespoons pine nuts or chopped pecans
1 clove garlic, minced
¼ teaspoon salt
   Dash ground red pepper
1 tablespoon olive oil or margarine
12 cups torn prewashed, fresh spinach
   (about 10 ounces)
1 tablespoon finely shredded Parmesan cheese

● In a kettle cook raisins, pine nuts or pecans, garlic, salt, and red pepper in hot oil over medium heat for 1 to 2 minutes or until garlic is light brown. Add spinach. Toss well to coat. Cook and stir for 2 minutes more or just until spinach is wilted and heated through. Sprinkle with Parmesan cheese before serving. Makes 4 servings.

Popeye Knows Best

Not only is spinach a good source of vitamins, but it's also low in calories. A whole cup of chopped fresh spinach contains just 10 calories; a ½ cup cooked has about 25 calories. Today it's easy to buy fresh prewashed spinach, which requires little work before using. If you don't buy it prewashed, however, be sure to wash it several times because the sand in which it is grown adheres to the leaves. To store fresh spinach, place the leaves in a plastic bag lined with a paper towel and keep it in the refrigerator for up to 3 days.

Country-Style Peas

Peas, ham, and onions combine here for a traditional Italian side dish. Stir in the nuts at the last moment to keep them crunchy.

1   ounce thinly sliced prosciutto or
    cooked ham
¼ cup chopped onion
1   teaspoon olive oil or cooking oil
1   10-ounce package frozen peas
¼ cup water
½ teaspoon instant chicken bouillon
    granules
¼ teaspoon dried oregano, crushed
    Dash pepper
2   tablespoons pine nuts or chopped
    walnuts, toasted

● Cut prosciutto or ham into thin strips. In a medium saucepan cook prosciutto or ham strips and onion in hot oil until onion is tender.

● Stir in the peas, water, bouillon granules, oregano, and pepper. Cover and simmer for 4 to 5 minutes or until peas are just tender. Stir in nuts. Makes 4 servings.

TOTAL FAT: 3 g
DAILY VALUE FAT: 4%
SATURATED FAT: 0 g
DAILY VALUE SATURATED FAT: 0%

NUTRITION FACTS
PER SERVING:

Calories	84
Total Fat	3 g
Saturated Fat	0 g
Cholesterol	3 mg
Sodium	241 mg
Carbohydrate	11 g
Fiber	4 g
Protein	5 g

EXCHANGES:
1 Starch
½ Fat

PREPARATION TIME: 10 minutes
COOKING TIME: 5 minutes

Cookies and Crema, recipe on page 149

Fresh Pear Custard Tart,
recipe on page 145

Desserts

We couldn't forget dessert, so we've included several to entice you, too. If you want a light dessert for a heavier meal, try the crisp and crunchy Chocolate Biscotti (page 144) with good, strong coffee for dunking. If decadence without guilt is your pleasure, Chocolate Swirl Cheesecake (page 152) is a must. But if elegance and style make you feel like a success in the kitchen, be sure to end your meal with Fresh Pear Custard Tart (page 145) to win everyone's applause.

TOTAL FAT: 3 g
DAILY VALUE FAT: 4%
SATURATED FAT: 2 g
DAILY VALUE SATURATED FAT: 10%

NUTRITION FACTS
PER SLICE BISCOTTI:

Calories	77
Total Fat	3 g
Saturated Fat	2 g
Cholesterol	18 mg
Sodium	54 mg
Carbohydrate	12 g
Fiber	1 g
Protein	1 g

EXCHANGES:
1 Starch
½ Fat

PREPARATION TIME: 28 minutes
BAKING TIME: 35 minutes
COOLING TIME: 1 hour

Chocolate Biscotti

These crunchy twice-baked cookies are delicious dipped in coffee or sweet wine. Using just a small amount of butter adds rich flavor but keeps fat content low—only 3 grams for each biscotti.

⅓ cup butter or margarine
⅔ cup sugar
¼ cup unsweetened cocoa powder
2 teaspoons baking powder
2 eggs
1¾ cups all-purpose flour
½ cup semisweet chocolate pieces or white
   baking pieces (optional)
1 teaspoon shortening (optional)

● In a large mixing bowl beat butter or margarine with an electric mixer on medium speed for 30 seconds or until softened. Add sugar, cocoa powder, and baking powder; beat until combined. Beat in eggs. Beat in as much of the flour as you can. Using a wooden spoon, stir in any remaining flour.

● Divide dough in half. On a lightly floured surface, shape each half into a 9-inch-long log. Place logs 5 inches apart on a lightly greased cookie sheet. Flatten logs until 2 inches wide.

● Bake in a 375° oven for 20 to 25 minutes or until a toothpick inserted near the center comes out clean. Cool on the cookie sheet on a wire rack for 1 hour. With a serrated knife, cut each log diagonally into ½-inch-thick slices. Lay slices, cut sides down, on an ungreased cookie sheet.

● Bake slices in a 325° oven for 8 minutes. Turn slices over. Bake 7 to 9 minutes more or until biscotti are dry and crisp (do not overbake). Cool thoroughly on a wire rack. If desired, melt chocolate or white baking pieces with shortening; drizzle over cooled cookies. Store biscotti in an airtight container at room temperature up to 1 week. Makes 32 slices.

Baking with Margarine

For baking, the Better Homes and Gardens® Test Kitchen suggests using a margarine that contains no less than 70 percent vegetable oil. Spreads that contain less vegetable oil and more water can affect the texture and overall quality of your baked goods. For example, biscotti made with an extra-light margarine or spread won't be as crisp as expected. When shopping, carefully read package labels (especially the fine print) to see how much vegetable oil is in the product.

Fresh Pear Custard Tart

Be sure to use ripe pears for this tart. Pears that are too firm or unripe will make it difficult to eat. If you're really in a pinch, substitute sliced, well-drained canned pears. (Pictured on pages 142 and 143.)

1 recipe Single-Crust Pastry
½ cup sugar
2 tablespoons cornstarch
2 cups skim milk
2 beaten eggs
4 teaspoons finely chopped crystallized
    ginger
1 teaspoon vanilla
⅔ cup pear nectar
1½ teaspoons cornstarch
3 small ripe pears
½ cup fresh berries (such as raspberries,
    blackberries, and/or blueberries)

● Prepare Single-Crust Pastry. For vanilla cream, in a heavy medium saucepan combine sugar and cornstarch. Stir in milk. Cook and stir over medium heat until mixture is thickened and bubbly. Cook and stir for 2 minutes more. Remove from heat. Gradually stir *about 1 cup* of the hot mixture into beaten eggs.

● Return all of the egg mixture to the saucepan. Stir in the ginger. Cook and stir until bubbly. Reduce heat. Cook and stir for 2 minutes more. Remove from heat. Stir in vanilla. Pour vanilla cream into baked pie shell. Cover and chill until ready to assemble.

● Meanwhile, for glaze, in a small saucepan combine the pear nectar and cornstarch. Cook and stir until thickened and bubbly. Cook and stir for 2 minutes more. Remove from heat. Cover and cool to room temperature.

● To assemble pie, peel, core, and thinly slice the pears. Arrange in a concentric pattern over the vanilla cream. Pour cooled glaze over pears, spreading evenly. Cover and chill 1 to 4 hours. To serve, top with berries. Makes 10 servings.

Single-Crust Pastry: In a medium mixing bowl stir together 1¼ cups *all-purpose flour* and ¼ teaspoon *salt*. Combine ¼ cup *skim milk* and 3 tablespoons *cooking oil*. Add oil mixture all at once to flour mixture. Stir with a fork until dough forms. Form dough into a ball.

● On a lightly floured surface, flatten the ball of dough with hands. Roll dough from center to the edge, forming a circle about 13 inches in diameter. Ease pastry into an 11-inch tart pan with removable bottom, being careful not to stretch the pastry. Trim pastry to the edge of the tart pan. Prick the bottom, sides, and corners of pastry generously with the tines of a fork. Bake in a 450° oven for 10 to 12 minutes or until pastry is golden. Cool in pan on a wire rack.

TOTAL FAT: 6 g
DAILY VALUE FAT: 9%
SATURATED FAT: 1 g
DAILY VALUE SATURATED FAT: 5%

**NUTRITION FACTS
PER SERVING:**

Calories	216
Total Fat	6 g
Saturated Fat	1 g
Cholesterol	44 mg
Sodium	96 mg
Carbohydrate	37 g
Fiber	2 g
Protein	5 g

EXCHANGES:
1 Starch
1½ Fruit
1 Fat

**PREPARATION TIME: 1 hour
CHILLING TIME: 1 hour**

TOTAL FAT: 5 g
DAILY VALUE FAT: 7%
SATURATED FAT: 2 g
DAILY VALUE SATURATED FAT: 10%

NUTRITION FACTS
PER SERVING:

Calories	136
Total Fat	5 g
Saturated Fat	2 g
Cholesterol	61 mg
Sodium	48 mg
Carbohydrate	19 g
Fiber	2 g
Protein	4 g

EXCHANGES:
1½ Fruit
1 Fat

PREPARATION TIME: 15 minutes
CHILLING TIME: 2 hours

Berries with Zabaglione

Similar to a custard sauce, zabaglione can be served with many desserts. This version contains a little sour cream for a slight tang.

2 tablespoons sugar
2 teaspoons cornstarch
¾ cup skim milk
1 beaten egg
¼ cup light dairy sour cream
2 tablespoons sweet or dry marsala
2 cups fresh berries (such as raspberries, blackberries, blueberries, or halved strawberries)
    Ground cinnamon or ground nutmeg

● For custard, in a heavy medium saucepan combine sugar and cornstarch. Stir in milk. Cook and stir over medium heat until mixture is thickened and bubbly. Cook and stir for 2 minutes more. Remove from heat. Gradually stir about half of the hot mixture into the beaten egg. Return all of the egg mixture to the saucepan. Cook until nearly bubbly, but *do not boil.* Immediately pour custard into a bowl; stir in sour cream and marsala. Cover the surface with plastic wrap. Chill the custard for 2 to 24 hours.

● To serve, divide the berries evenly among 4 dessert dishes. Spoon custard evenly over the berries. Sprinkle with cinnamon or nutmeg. Serve immediately. Makes 4 servings.

Fruit Finales

Health experts recommend eating five or more servings of fruits or vegetables per day. Although that may seem like a lot, with a little planning you can easily meet the goal. One of the more pleasurable ways to serve fruits is in scrumptious desserts, such as the one above. If you like to close your meal with something sweet, plan on serving fruit-based desserts a couple times a week. Don't forget that naturally sweet fresh fruit can stand on its own as a mealtime finale.

TOTAL FAT: 4 g
DAILY VALUE FAT: 6%
SATURATED FAT: 1 g
DAILY VALUE SATURATED FAT: 5%

NUTRITION FACTS
PER SERVING:

Calories	150
Total Fat	4 g
Saturated Fat	1 g
Cholesterol	57 mg
Sodium	46 mg
Carbohydrate	27 g
Fiber	1 g
Protein	2 g

EXCHANGES:
1 Starch
½ Fruit
1 Fat

PREPARATION TIME: 40 minutes
BAKING TIME: 20 minutes

Caramelized Apple Wedges

Thin apple bars are a traditional treat in Florence during Epiphany.

1 tablespoon butter or margarine
2 large cooking apples (such as Granny Smith), peeled, cored, and very thinly sliced
¼ cup sugar
2 eggs
½ cup sugar
2 tablespoons all-purpose flour
2 tablespoons lemon juice
1 tablespoon water
¼ teaspoon baking powder
¼ teaspoon ground cinnamon
  Nonstick spray coating
¼ cup toasted sliced almonds
  Powdered sugar (optional)

● In a large skillet melt the butter or margarine. Add the apples and the ¼ cup sugar. Cook over medium heat for 15 to 20 minutes or until apples are golden, stirring occasionally.

● Meanwhile, in a small bowl combine the eggs, the ½ cup sugar, the flour, lemon juice, water, baking powder, and cinnamon. Beat with an electric mixer on medium speed for 2 minutes or until thoroughly combined.

● Spray a 9-inch pie plate with nonstick coating. Arrange cooked apple slices in pie plate. Sprinkle almonds over apples. Pour egg mixture over apple mixture.

● Bake in a 350° oven about 20 minutes or until it is lightly browned around the edges and center is set. Cool on a wire rack. Serve warm or chilled. If desired, sift powdered sugar over top. Cut into wedges to serve. Makes 8 servings.

Cookies and Crema

This dessert usually is made with whipping cream and yogurt. To lighten the calorie load, we skipped the cream and yogurt and added fat-free sour cream to light dessert topping instead. We also used slice-and-bake cookies instead of a homemade pastry to save you time. (Pictured on page 142.)

¼ of a 20-ounce roll refrigerated sugar cookie dough, sliced ¼ inch thick (8 slices)
½ cup light, frozen whipped dessert topping, thawed
½ cup fat-free dairy sour cream
1 teaspoon finely shredded orange peel
3 cups fresh or frozen berries (such as raspberries, blackberries, or sliced strawberries) thawed and drained
Unsweetened cocoa powder (optional)
Fresh mint leaves (optional)

● Bake cookies according to package directions. Set aside to cool.

● Meanwhile, combine the dessert topping and sour cream. Stir in the shredded orange peel. Cover and chill until serving time.

● To assemble, place a cookie on each of 4 dessert plates. Top each cookie with *one-fourth* of the berries; top with *one-fourth* of the sour cream mixture (about ¼ cup) and another cookie. If desired, sift cocoa powder lightly over each and garnish with mint. Makes 4 servings.

Clouds of Cream

Whipped cream contains lots of calories and fat. Today, there are many choices on the market to satisfy your love of whipped cream. Compare these options for a 2-tablespoon serving:

	Calories	Fat (g)	Saturated Fat (g)
Whipped cream	52	6	4
Frozen whipped dessert topping	25	2	2
Light, frozen whipped dessert topping	20	1	1
Nonfat, frozen whipped dessert topping	15	0	0

TOTAL FAT: 7 g
DAILY VALUE FAT: 10%
SATURATED FAT: 3 g
DAILY VALUE SATURATED FAT: 15%

NUTRITION FACTS PER SERVING:

Calories	222
Total Fat	7 g
Saturated Fat	3 g
Cholesterol	5 mg
Sodium	154 mg
Carbohydrate	36 g
Fiber	4 g
Protein	3 g

EXCHANGES:
1 Starch
1 Fruit
1 Fat

PREPARATION TIME: 20 minutes
BAKING TIME: 8 minutes

Tiramisu

We've simplified the classic tiramisu (tee-rah-MEE-su) by using a purchased angel food cake. Most important, it's as light as a feather. Just by using lower-fat products, this slimmer version saves 14 grams fat and 200 calories per serving from the original recipe.

1   8-ounce package light cream cheese (Neufchâtel), softened
½   cup sifted powdered sugar
3   tablespoons coffee liqueur
1   8-ounce container light, frozen whipped dessert topping, thawed
¼   cup fat-free dairy sour cream
2   tablespoons coffee liqueur
1   8- to 10-inch round angel food cake
¼   cup strong black coffee
2   tablespoons coffee liqueur
1   recipe Mocha Fudge Sauce (optional)

● For filling, in a large bowl combine the cream cheese, powdered sugar, and the 3 tablespoons liqueur; beat with an electric mixer on medium speed until blended and smooth. Stir in ½ cup of the whipped dessert topping. Set aside.

● For the frosting, in another bowl combine the remaining whipped dessert topping, the sour cream, and 2 tablespoons liqueur. Set aside.

● Using a serrated knife, cut the angel food cake horizontally into 3 layers. Place 1 layer on a serving platter and 2 layers on large dinner plates. With a long-tined fork or a skewer, poke holes in tops of all 3 layers. In a small bowl combine the coffee and 2 tablespoons liqueur; drizzle over all layers. Spread the first layer with *half* of the filling. Add a second layer and spread on the remaining filling. Add top layer of cake. Frost cake with the frosting. (If desired, cover and chill for up to 4 hours.)

● If desired, just before serving, drizzle top and sides with Mocha Fudge Sauce. To serve, drizzle dessert plates with more sauce (if desired), cut cake into wedges, and top with a cake slice. Makes 16 servings.

Mocha Fudge Sauce: In a small bowl dissolve 1 teaspoon *instant coffee crystals* in 1 teaspoon *hot water;* stir in ¼ cup *chocolate-flavored syrup.*

TOTAL FAT: 7 g
DAILY VALUE FAT: 10%
SATURATED FAT: 3 g
DAILY VALUE SATURATED FAT: 15%

NUTRITION FACTS
PER SERVING:

Calories	151
Total Fat	7 g
Saturated Fat	3 g
Cholesterol	18 mg
Sodium	195 mg
Carbohydrate	17 g
Fiber	0 g
Protein	6 g

EXCHANGES:
1 Starch
½ Lean Meat
1 Fat

PREPARATION TIME: 15 minutes
BAKING TIME: 30 minutes
COOLING TIME: 2 hours
CHILLING TIME: 4 hours

Chocolate Swirl Cheesecake

Low-fat cottage cheese and light cream cheese are the secret ingredients that keep fat and calories low in this creamy cheesecake. Enjoy a slice with a cup of cappuccino or espresso.

⅓ **cup crushed chocolate wafers (about 7)**
1 **cup low-fat cottage cheese**
1 **8-ounce package light cream cheese (Neufchâtel)**
¾ **cup sugar**
1 **teaspoon vanilla**
½ **cup refrigerated or frozen egg product, thawed, or 2 eggs**
3 **tablespoons unsweetened cocoa powder**
3 **tablespoons water**
  Fanned strawberry halves or fresh raspberries (optional)

● Sprinkle wafer crumbs evenly in the bottom of an 8-inch springform pan. Set aside.

● Place the cottage cheese in a food processor bowl or blender container; cover and process or blend until smooth. Add cream cheese, sugar, and vanilla. Process or blend until combined. (Mixture will be thick; scrape the sides of the bowl, if necessary.)

● Transfer cheese mixture to a large mixing bowl. Stir in the egg product or eggs. Pour *half* of the mixture into the crumb-lined pan. In a small bowl dissolve cocoa powder in the water. Stir the chocolate mixture into the remaining cheese mixture. Carefully pour the chocolate mixture over the plain mixture in the pan.*

● Bake in a 300° oven for 30 to 35 minutes or until center appears nearly set when gently shaken. Cool on a wire rack for 10 minutes to be sure cheesecake doesn't crack. Loosen side of pan. Cool 30 minutes more; remove side of pan. Cool completely. Cover and chill several hours or overnight. If desired, decorate the top of the cheesecake with strawberries or raspberries. Makes 12 servings.

Note: If desired, instead of dividing batter, dissolve chocolate in water and add to cheesecake mixture along with egg product or eggs. This will give a light-colored chocolate cheesecake.

Crespelle with Orange Sauce

Crespelle (krehs-PEHL-lay) are the Italian equivalents of crepes. Prepare the thin pancakes ahead of time and refrigerate or freeze between layers of waxed paper. Thaw crepes at room temperature about an hour before using.

⅓ cup sugar
3 tablespoons all-purpose flour
½ teaspoon finely shredded orange peel
¼ teaspoon salt
1¼ cups skim milk
1 beaten egg or ¼ cup refrigerated or frozen egg product, thawed
1 teaspoon butter or margarine
1 teaspoon vanilla
½ teaspoon finely shredded orange peel
1 cup orange juice
⅓ cup golden raisins
¼ cup sugar
1 recipe Crespelle

● For filling, in a medium saucepan combine the ⅓ cup sugar, the flour, ½ teaspoon orange peel, and the salt. Stir in milk. Cook and stir until thickened and bubbly. Cook and stir 2 minutes more. Gradually stir *half* of the hot mixture into egg or egg product. Return all of egg mixture to saucepan. Cook and stir just until bubbly. Remove from heat. Stir in butter or margarine and vanilla; cover surface with plastic wrap. Cool without stirring.

● For sauce, in a small saucepan combine the ½ teaspoon orange peel, orange juice, raisins, and the ¼ cup sugar. Bring to boiling; reduce heat. Cover and simmer for 5 minutes. Set aside. Prepare Crespelle. Spread about *1 tablespoon* of the filling over unbrowned side of each Crespelle, leaving ¼-inch rim around edge. Roll up, jelly-roll style. Place, seam sides down, in greased 2-quart rectangular baking dish, forming 2 layers; pour sauce over tops. Cover and bake in 375° oven about 15 minutes. Makes 8 servings.

Crespelle: Combine 1 cup *all-purpose flour;* 1½ cups *skim milk;* ½ cup refrigerated or frozen *egg product,* thawed; 2 tablespoons *sugar;* 1 tablespoon *cooking oil;* and ⅛ teaspoon *salt.* Beat with rotary beater until blended. Heat a lightly greased nonstick 6-inch skillet. Remove from heat. Spoon in *2 tablespoons* batter; lift and tilt skillet to spread batter. Return to heat; brown on 1 side. Invert pan over paper towels; remove Crespelle. Repeat to make 16 to 18, greasing skillet as needed.

Berry Crespelle: Prepare Crespelle as above, *except,* for sauce, omit raisins. Before serving, sprinkle with ⅓ cup *fresh raspberries.*

TOTAL FAT: 5 g
DAILY VALUE FAT: 7%
SATURATED FAT: 1 g
DAILY VALUE SATURATED FAT: 5%

NUTRITION FACTS
PER SERVING:

Calories	254
Total Fat	5 g
Saturated Fat	1 g
Cholesterol	30 mg
Sodium	187 mg
Carbohydrate	45 g
Fiber	1 g
Protein	8 g

EXCHANGES:
2 Starch
1 Fruit
½ Fat

PREPARATION TIME: 35 minutes
BAKING TIME: 15 minutes

We've taken the hassle out of planning a tasty meal for you and your family. Here's more than a week's worth of menus to get you started on eating low-fat meals—the Italian way.

Chicken with Golden Raisins, page 79
Steamed baby carrots
Baked Potatoes with Mushrooms, page 132
Cookies and Crema, page 149

Vegetable Lasagna with Red Pepper Sauce, page 122
Steamed yellow wax beans
Easy Herb Focaccia, page 54
Crespelle with Orange Sauce, page 153

Pizza Rustica, p. 60
Country-Style Peas, p. 141
Mixed greens salad
Berries with Zabaglione, page 146

Shrimp-Artichoke Frittata, page 114
Zucchini alla Romana, page 138
Pepper-Cheese Bread, page 57
Fresh Pear Custard Tart, p. 145

Pasta alla Carbonara with Asparagus, page 84
Country Whole Wheat Bread, page 58
Tiramisu, page 150

Whole Wheat Pesto Pizza, page 62
Mixed greens salad with vinaigrette
Chocolate Biscotti, page 144

Make-Ahead Minestrone, page 36
Panzanella, page 18
Chocolate Swirl Cheesecake, page 152

Fresh Tomato Soup with Tortellini, page 35
Pepper and Cheese Sandwich, page 57
Caramelized Apple Wedges, page 148

Metric Cooking Hints

By making a few conversions, cooks in Australia, Canada, and the United Kingdom can use the recipes in *Better Homes and Gardens® Low-fat & Luscious Italian* with confidence. The charts on this page provide a guide for converting measurements from the U.S. customary system, which is used throughout this book, to the imperial and metric systems. There also is a conversion table for oven temperatures to accommodate the differences in oven calibrations.

Volume and Weight: Americans traditionally use cup measures for liquid and solid ingredients. The chart (top right) shows the approximate imperial and metric equivalents. If you are accustomed to weighing solid ingredients, here are some helpful approximate equivalents.

● 1 cup butter, castor sugar, or rice = 8 ounces = about 250 grams
● 1 cup flour = 4 ounces = about 125 grams
● 1 cup icing sugar = 5 ounces = about 150 grams

Spoon measures are used for smaller amounts of ingredients. Although the size of the tablespoon varies slightly among countries, for practical purposes and for recipes in this book, a straight substitution is all that's necessary.

Measurements made using cups or spoons should always be level, unless stated otherwise.

Product Differences: Most of the ingredients called for in the recipes in this book are available in English-speaking countries. However, some are known by different names. Here are some common American ingredients and the possible counterparts:

● Sugar is granulated or castor sugar.
● Powdered sugar is icing sugar.
● All-purpose flour is plain household flour or white flour. When self-rising flour is used in place of all-purpose flour in a recipe that calls for leavening, omit the leavening agent (baking soda or baking powder) and salt.
● Light corn syrup is golden syrup.
● Cornstarch is cornflour.
● Baking soda is bicarbonate of soda.
● Vanilla is vanilla essence.

Useful Equivalents

⅛ teaspoon = 0.5 millilitre
¼ teaspoon = 1 millilitre
½ teaspoon = 2 millilitre
1 teaspoon = 5 millilitre
¼ cup = 2 fluid ounces = 50 millilitre
⅓ cup = 3 fluid ounces = 75 millilitre
½ cup = 4 fluid ounces = 125 millilitre

⅔ cup = 5 fluid ounces = 150 millilitre
¾ cup = 6 fluid ounces = 175 millilitre
1 cup = 8 fluid ounces = 250 millilitre
2 cups = 1 pint
2 pints = 1 litre
½ inch = 1 centimetre
1 inch = 2 centimetres

Baking Pan Sizes

American	Metric
8×1½-inch round baking pan	20×4-centimetre sandwich or cake tin
9×1½-inch round baking pan	23×3.5-centimetre sandwich or cake tin
11×7×1½-inch baking pan	28×18×4-centimetre baking pan
13×9×2-inch baking pan	32.5×23×5-centimetre baking pan
2-quart-rectangular baking dish	30×19×5-centimetre baking pan
15×10×2-inch baking pan	38×25.5×2.5-centimetre baking pan (Swiss roll tin)
9-inch pie plate	22×4- or 23×4-centimetre pie plate
7- or 8-inch springform pan	18- or 20-centimetre springform or loose-bottom cake tin
9×5×3-inch loaf pan narrow loaf pan or paté tin	23×13×6-centimetre or 2-pound
1½-quart casserole	1.5-litre casserole
2-quart casserole	2-litre casserole

Oven Temperature Equivalents

Fahrenheit Setting	Celsius Setting*	Gas
300°F	150°C	Gas Mark 2
325°F	160°C	Gas Mark 3
350°F	180°C	Gas Mark 4
375°F	190°C	Gas Mark 5
400°F	200°C	Gas Mark 6
425°F	220°C	Gas Mark 7
450°F	230°C	Gas Mark 8
Broil		Grill

Electric and gas ovens may be calibrated using Celsius. However, increase the Celsius setting 10 to 20 degrees when cooking above 160°C with an electric oven. For convection or forced-air ovens (gas or electric), lower the temperature setting 10°C when cooking at all heat levels.

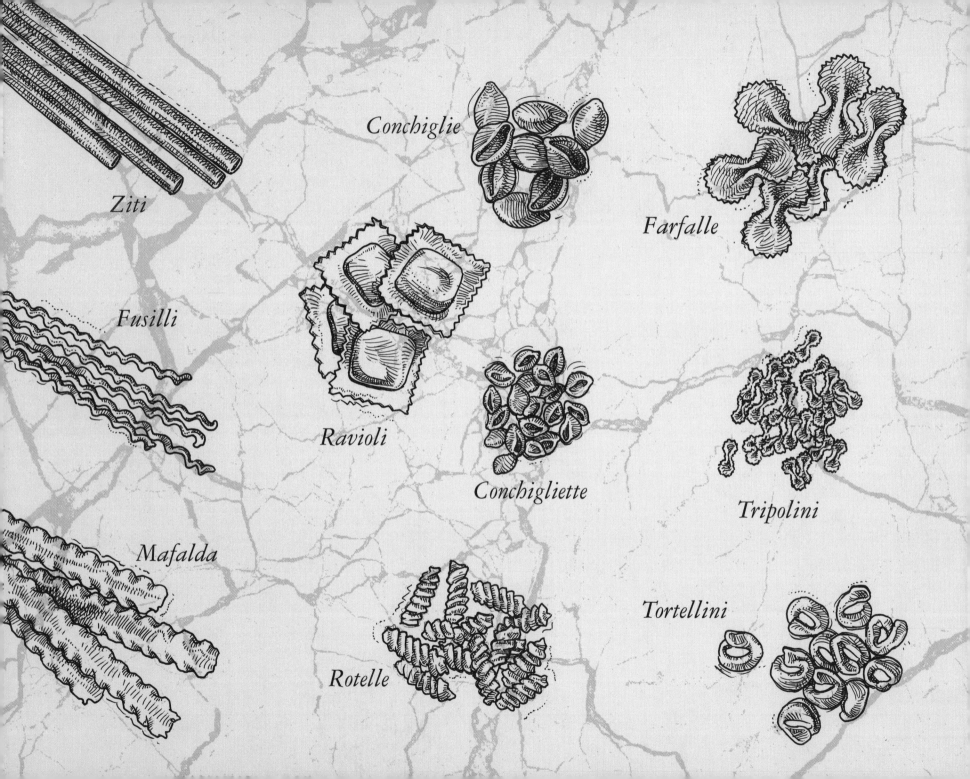

Ziti

Conchiglie

Farfalle

Fusilli

Ravioli

Conchigliette

Tripolini

Mafalda

Tortellini

Rotelle